Vijay & Sheila

Destination America

A Novel in Verse

Hanu Rao

Vijay and Sheila is a work of fiction. Unless otherwise indicated, all the names, characters, businesses, institutions, places, events and incidents in this book are either the product of the author's imagination or used in a fictitious manner. Any resemblance to actual persons, living or dead, or actual events is purely coincidental.

To Kanthamani, my dear wife and lifemate.

Contents

Preface

This book provides a rare look at the under-belly of a great nation—the United States of America. Instead of the historically celebrated, well-lit tourist spots which attract people from all over the world, the book takes the reader on a tour of prisons, inner city schools, and other urban locales, with "flat-out foreigners" serving as tour guides.

The reactions of newcomers over the generations, as they personally discover America, are hardly new. However, the protagonists in this fantasy—brand new arrivals from India—find themselves, by dint of their jobs, in the unusual and challenging position of having to probe deep into the bowels of society, places removed from the mainstream. Sheila is invited from far away India to work as a math teacher in an inner city school, while her husband, Vijay, finds work as a psychologist in a state prison. The jobs drag them right away into the thick of entrenched urban problems, overwhelming the new arrivals. As the ever sensible and practical Sheila remarks, "...besides, what can we do, brand-new immigrants, barely tolerated, other than do our jobs as sincerely as we can."

This book also delves into the psychology of the more recent immigrants to the U.S. These modern-day immigrants from India are well prepared for 21st-century America, thanks to their facility in English and the professional education they bring with them. Coming from *"the land of bustling bazaars and buffalo chips, these sons and daughters of India descend into the valley of Silicon chips...they are the scientists, engineers and doctors...they're the drained brains from distant shores..."* These so-called high-tech immigrants are attaining instant success in the U.S., professionally and financially. This book is an attempt to document the typical reactions such a pre-selected group of immigrants experiences, when they settle down to live in America. We learn how they tend to be picky in choosing from the American social menu, as many items leave them feeling perplexed and threatened. Their preconceived and unreasonable expectations of America make the visitors wary of some practices towards which they were perfectly indifferent when the very same occurred back in their native lands. Thus, as Vijay, the protagonist-psychologist, observes "They *look around and see America, with all aspects unveiled. Everything is magnified to the bug-eyed visitor. The good is very good, even awe-inspiring, while the bad is repulsive, thanks to media graphics."*

The new arrivals appreciate the American society's comprehensive constitutional framework which allows responsible speech and expression, and other basic protections. The psychological process of gradual assimilation and American identity is also described.

It shows how the newcomer takes time to overcome his or her initial puzzlement, even resistance, before realizing the greatness and prudence of the American system.

Finally, a word about the use of verse instead of prose.

The dramatic scenes in the book required the power that could only be supplied by lines of verse, "instead of plodding prose." It took all the language skills, imagination, drama, and humor at the author's disposal to describe "the doings and goings on in the magnet nation of modern man..."

Let's not miss the magic
of the moment,
so easy to overlook
what's right beneath our nose.
That I can write this using
not an owl's quill, but
a roller ball containing
non-fading black gel,
conveying a mild sense of thrill
at recollected reflections,
half real, half chimerical.
Sharing thrill and pouring out
my soul on paper, which cost
but a penny and pen, hardly
a Japanese Yen!
That you and I are happening
at all, my, what magic!

Castlegate Correctional Center

The story of Paul Milholland, an inmate serving prison time for DWI-related Manslaughter, introduces one of the protagonists, Dr. Vijay Bhaskar, a newly arrived psychologist from India, as he orients himself to his work in the field of corrections.

1
They have a story to tell
and a song to sing!
No rhyme nor ratified reason
will give them pause.
These characters are
waiting in the wings,
ready to roll—to roll
out the ballad.
Bit players in borrowed
costumes can't wait
for the band to break out.
They could be a bit crude
and just a tad lewd,
truth be told. A few
given to rancor, *caveat emptor*!
You see, many were done in
before they could find
a finishing school.

2
Castlegate Correctional Center
wakes up in a slow canter,
naked bodies stumbling out
of beds made of Pennsylvania steel.

The start of a new day,
it already has a worn-out feel.
The unswerving routine,
suffice to say,
is designed to keep
the denizens at bay.
Black, White, and Hispanic,
Red Man and the occasional
Oriental, all live
in coerced comity,
duly convicted and condemned
by a diligent and just dispensary.

3
"Paul Milholland! Where
the hell is he?"
bellows the Rodent, the fat
road-squad sergeant,
scratching irritably at his
newly acquired goatee.
"He is hittin' the can, big man!
Reckon last night's beans
have hit the fan!"
offers a clown,
raising brief laughter
in the back of the
prison pickup-van.
Paul hurries out
zipping up his pants,
and piles himself onboard,
just as the truck rolls out
into the hot, humid morning,
the cargo in the Fargo
quietly mourning.

4

Back in the joint, seeking
escape in prison
from the sweltering work
of hacking foliage
along Route. 101,
picking deer ticks
with a plastic fork,
Paul declares to no one
in particular:
"I don't wish this upon any man,
enemy or friend!
Lord, this place is nothing,
if not pure hell . . ."
Old Jim in the next bunk
rolls over laughing,
saying, "Take it easy pal,
you can go on and on,
but this place will be around
for the long haul…
well after you and I
disappear in its pall!"

5

"Mr. Milholland, I'm Dr. Bhaskar.
It says here, you haven't
been feeling too well?"
"Yes, that's the God-honest
truth, good doctor.
Can't sleep a wink;
too many worries to tell.
The body here, mind out there.
This ain't no place
for a grown man;

not someone who was
the head of his clan."
"Exactly, what's the crime
which fetched you all this
time, Mr. Milholland?"
"From the barstool to the car,
a drunken fool, I stumbled.
Keys went in the ignition,
is all I remember.
Next thing, the bodies
lay all dismembered;
a pregnant woman and her
three-year-old,
I was later told."

6
"God-fearing colored folks,
on their way home
from a late-night
revival in the cold.
I've had breaks on many a DUI,
lucky to hit the brakes
and not collide.
In the end, every dog
will meet its fate;
sooner or later, your
name comes up on the slate."
"Well, Paul, if I may so you call,
how do you feel about the two,
actually, three; who died?"
"Why, I just feel terrible.
Is there anything more horrible?
Doin' in a pregnant woman
and her innocent little young 'un?"

But the good Lord
did cut me some slack;
I was filled with
repentance, so
they spared me
the death sentence!

7
Welcome to the Deep South,
Veeragandham Vijay Bhaskar!
This is unlike anything you've seen
in the land of *Surya Namaskar*.
While they sit on the same global band,
give or take a few degrees of latitude,
The Dixieland and *Dakshin Khand,*
what a difference in attitude!
The East is East, the West is West,
one is into doing with the least,
the other into what's very best;
indeed, the twain shall never meet,
even as the planes criss-cross,
with engines emitting
the globalization drumbeat!

A Many Splendored Drama

The poet introduces the subject—tales of
fallible human beings—and the unfettered
spirit in which the verse is written.

8
Thus begins this story,
set in our time in history,
addressed to all and sundry.
One needeth but
a sense rudimentary,
and compassion for
a poet's lamentary!
Rhyme and rhythm
go only so far,
useless if one were
to venture too far.
We shall not stress
the rules of meter,
which won't get us
past St. Peter!
Let free-floating thoughts
convey, as only
they can purvey,
unconstrained by
the purist's duress.

9
Feeling and emotion,
context and connotation,
furrowed frown or guttural groan,
peals of laughter or whatever
one is after,

fly best when set free.
In such unfettered
spirit, we'll immerse
in the permissive realms of free verse!

10
This tale is a recounting
of human affairs.
An acrimonious, heterogeneous
depository of homo sapiens
in need of repair.
Man bites dog and runs
into the night, howling.
Another, a man of cloth,
gives in to common sloth
and goes bowling with his loveling.
People, places, and times
mark these scatterphrenic rhymes,
ringing the bells and chimes,
proclaiming till eternity,
the dubious human fraternity!

11
Our concern in this vast
scheme—so vast that it
keeps unfolding like
Draupadi's Sari of Modesty,
unending and eternal,
like day after night,
after day; sun-rise, after
sun-set, after sun-rise,
to keep up with which
the billion-odd neurons
in the bitty blob of

grey matter hardly suffice—
our concern is with two
little souls, two finite,
fleshy and fickle creatures,
making the most of
their one-act *Hangama*,
in this marvelous
many-splendored drama!

In the Middle of a Color-Coded Superpower!

A short segment that touches on Vijay and Sheila's initial reception upon landing on US soil and how they adapt to their new surroundings in America.

12
Vijay and Sheila are our quarries,
as we pursue them
like shameless voyeurs,
in their hours together
and those spent
on their own in the name
of their chosen professions,
expressly for which
they were imported
from across the world;
from a hot, dusty, and
crowded land,
to a cold, clean,
free-choice land.
From the brightest jewel in
the British Crown,
to the crown jewel
of Modern Man;
from the largest and
bustlingest democracy,
to a vibrant, willful technocracy.
They skipped over Silk Road,
riding the friendly skies,
until they landed at JFK
and processed by
government guys.

13
Two years have passed
since Vijay & Sheila migrated;
not before they were hassled
and duly denigrated
by the consul, customs,
and travel agents,
on embarkation and destination.
Just another pair of do-gooders,
who landed with their
marching orders.
"How many bags? What's inside?
Have you touched a leper
in the last day after supper?
Do you carry pickles made of
mustard seed and peppers?
Welcome to the United States,
you suckers for the almighty dollar!"
Whatever, sir...
bottom line...at the
end of the day...
here they are,
our two players,
right in the middle of
of the coveted,
color-coded superpower!

14
Sheila, whose real name
is Suseela (Sanskrit for one
with a good moral character),
is up early, cooking
the breakfast barley.
The cold-water shower

did give her the shivers,
but tested her
willpower just barely.
Such sober, sensible habits
have always won her plaudits,
back in the Land of the Hermits.

15
It's Saturday morning
in the suburbs,
her mate's sleeping late.
Not being one
who disturbs,
she grabs the phone
from its crate,
and walks out onto the balcony,
for her weekly, prepaid,
international telephony.
"Life in the USA?
Chennagidde, baagundi: it's fine!"
Their vernaculated voices
are carried across
the earth's horizon,
thanks to the brainy folks
behind cellular Verizon.

Quite a Place, This America!

The short poem recognizes America as the most desired immigration destination on the planet.

16
Quite a place this America!
Renowned for its creativity
and human ingenuity;
people flock to it
for it's the material Mecca.
Its citizenry is spirited
with sheer audacity,
ill at ease
with any ambiguity.
Down to earth, up to date,
and at the ready,
nations send
their teams to make a study;
of its icons and institutions,
which leaves them heady.
One despairs
it's naïve optimism,
till one watches them
bunny-hopping on the moon!
The home ground of Tarzan,
Superman, and Disneystan,
it's a place always
on the run and nonstop fun.
Such is the Land of Lincoln,
the late-model sports sedan!

They Build a Nest

Sheila first and then Vijay find employment in the United States—she with the struggling public school system and he with the prison system.

17
Sheila and Vijay quickly build a nest,
a base to play the 9 to 5
and slowly prosper.
Trained as a math teacher
who can help arrest
the alarming dropout rate
from the school roster,
Sheila was the first to go out,
to go win some bread,
while Vijay looked on, peeking
through the window
with a tinge of envy,
and quite a bit of dread.
But he didn't have
to spend too much time
lying low, thanks to
the skyrocketing crime boom.
Drug infestations and
gang manifestations
sent hordes of young
black men to an early doom.
Vijay was hired by a desperate
prison administration,
to please come in
and sort out the rotten apples
from the all-but-forgotten oranges.

An Arranged Marriage!

A semi-humorous segment that describes
how Vijay and Sheila were originally brought
together purely by the efforts of their parents
back in India. Following the wedding, Vijay
follows Sheila, who is offered a teaching
position in a US High School.

18
Vijay met Sheila
through an ad
in the *Bangalore Banner*,
as too much work
and social inhibition
left things pretty much
up to his dad,
who launched a campaign,
even attended
an exhibition where
boy meets girl,
and after a few clock ticks,
the boy decides
and the girl acquiesces!

19
Vijay was shown many
a Four by Six
of hopeful damsels
and insistent ingénues;
two-dimensional renderings
of those from the opposite sex,
who submit themselves
for the verdict, through

paper and email review.
Do you like what you see,
does she meet the specs?
Be sure to check her eyes:
hope, despair, or worse,
defiance, what's the key?!
Some with chubby cheeks
and broken teeth,
a few with long, slender necks.
Does she seem
charming and disarming,
or too sober and sulky?
Is she fair and fancy-looking,
or plain, swarthy, and bulky?

20
There, the weighty issue
of slimness...
Is she slender
as a salamander?
or a buxom broad,
like an overfed
Madrasi movie star?
Or, oh well, how'd you say it,
just too fat to pass
through the colander?!
Questions, impressions,
and summary judgments
from afar, a stimulus-response
Pavlovian salivaction.

21
"Perhaps she'll make
the right impression.

Then again, who can tell?
I might develop an aversion,
in which case I hate
to cause her depression."
In the end, Vijay was like
"Oh, my God, Dad,
this one is so beautiful!
She's tall, slim, and fair.
Tender like a mid-
summer daffodil,
with long, slender fingers,
and raven-black hair!
OK, Dad, let's meet this princess
in person for up-close inspection,
to determine if it'll
lead to any real action!"

22
"Hey, Dad, can I ask her questions?"
"Certainly, son. I'm sure
Sheila's Dad wouldn't mind,
would you, Dr. Murthy?"
"Absolutely, yes! I mean,
absolutely not!" blurted out
Prof. Manjunath Murthy,
feeling like a dope for his
Freudian fumbling.
"Actually, the youngsters
may proceed to the Cubbon Park.
My car and driver are waiting,
as a matter of fact."
offered Dr. Murthy,
recovering his tact.
Sheila joined Vijay,

after a show of diffidence,
which met with approval
from Vijay's Puritan parents.

23
Vijay pats the family pooch,
asleep on the porch.
He is deliriously happy,
as if he's had some hooch.
Climbing in the car after her,
he's feeling he's won
the Mysore State Lottery,
while Sheila's wondering
if this also goes
the way of broken pottery.

24
"Well, I know you must be
feeling quite awkward.
This whole process
is so very backward,"
Vijay tried to break the ice.
Sheila turned her head,
and, looking directly at him,
said, "I'm sorry, I may be
a bit too forward.
Everything happens for a reason,
and nothing happens out of season.
I strongly believe that
all this is a matter
of male domination, nothing
but female subjugation!"

25
Vijay was unnerved
at the directness
of her response,
never mind the imported
inter-sex invective.
Alarming as her position was,
he's quite taken with
her contra-diplomatic candor,
which only added to
his aggravated ardor.
He looked at her and confessed:
"Sheila, men folk do
tend to be coarse
and insensitive, in general,
ignoring a woman's susceptibilities."

26
They're sitting on a park bench,
not far from the imposing statue
of Lord General Cubbon,
mounted on a black
gun-metal horse.
Men, thought Sheila—
fiddling with her ribbon—
when will they learn
to be honest and speak
their mind? Women, thought
Vijay—stealing sideward
glances—how lovely they look;
this one in particular,
I best hurry and book!

27
Vijay quickly decides,
Sheila's the one for him.
First of all, she is comely,
pert, and lovely.
She's modern—more Western,
that's for certain.
Plus, she's a teacher of maths,
crucial for all different paths!
What's more, she's cast
from the same mold,
falling within the
fastidious Brahmin fold.
This arranged marriage
business works for Vijay.
No dates, hassles, or debacles.
Who cares for conquests
and contests? Too much
self-indulgence leads to
ego disturbance, they say.
Leave it to the
elders; they've overcome
many steep boulders.
He doesn't mind, in the least,
riding on their shoulders!

28
For her part, Sheila surmised
that this latest suitor,
who could be a bit more cuter,
doesn't seem like a bad sort.
"But what's with daddy this,
and daddy that?
Please, he is supposed to be

a psychologist, for Freud's sake!
Wonder, what kind of complex
does he have to be so
dependent on the Patriarch?
Don't tell me he's
still afraid of the dark!
Well, be that as it may.
After all, life's a package deal.
They may have all four wheels,
but missing the steering wheel!
So, I'm going to say yes
to this deal and not prolong the ordeal."

29
They set a summer date
and time. Never mind
the heat and grime.
Early hours are
the most auspicious,
decreed the *Purohit*,
with an air somewhat suspicious.
They showed up for the wedding
from all corners,
carrying kids and bedding.
It was a two-day affair,
full of pomp and flair,
culminating with Vijay,
standing over Sheila suitably seated
on soft silk cushions,
tying the Holy Knot
around her long, slender neck—
not once, not twice, but thrice
for good measure.
They placed on each other's heads,

the bitter-sweet concoction
of *jaggery* and *cumin seed*,
and poured yellow Jasmine rice
over each other's heads while
the spectators cried, "Nice, nice!"

30
It was Sheila who got the invite,
to come and teach
kids stateside,
those lagging behind
in math and science.
Incredible in a land
from whence they
daily launch
laser-rocket appliances!
Sheila visited the
visa office, where Vijay
was tagged onto her passport.
In line with Vijay's trepidations,
the consul advised him
to lower his employment
expectations. While surely
there are
enough American slouches,
there are
more than enough
money-metered couches.
"But not to lose heart, Dr. Bhaskar.
We're getting crazier
by the day! There'll be
plenty coming your way."

Sheila Reports to MLK High

Sheila Bhaskar, the newly imported tenth-grade math teacher, reports to work. The experiences and impressions she gains on her first day on the job in America are viewed through the confused and critical eyes of a newly arrived foreign worker.

31
A certified novice,
Sheila entered the American traffic,
ignoring bumper sticker
graphics, anxiously
adhering to the driving code.
Yet, a road-side scene—of a mother-child team,
trying to board a school bus
stopped right in front of Sheila—
pulled her into a poetic reverie.

32
It's early October,
the leaves still hesitant to fall;
and little children, reluctant
to climb on the yellow school bus.
Reluctant, afraid, and sad
to leave the safety and
sap of motherly love.
Who wants to leave
the high perch, where it's
always nice and breezy?
And fall to the ground,
however softly, in

shattering disillusionment?
To move on
and march towards
measured inevitability.

33
Sheila parked her car,
careful to avoid a tow-away.
The rows and rows
of parked cars
gleamed while they
waited faithfully
for the reluctant day scholars,
learning to make the dollars.
She walked towards
the school entrance,
trying to shake that
feeling of inevitability.

34
Not a soul outside,
can you believe it?!
Sheila addressed her secret self,
who alone sympathized
with her cultural struggles.
The large brick structure
seemed like it swallowed
the children whole,
most of whom are on the dole.
It's a crime punishable
by time, they said,
for a kid to skip school,
because that's just not cool.
Time in jail or time

in a government school,
one is free to pick
one's own pastime!

35
Sheila passed by the flags
in the front, fluttering stiffly
in the breeze, not knowing
whether to stop and salute
the many stars and several stripes,
steeped in red, white, and blue.
The flags seemed to
reprimand her: "Beware
you migrant, we want
you to feel welcome,
but don't take things
for granted. Work hard,
only then play hard.
Workaholism first, only
then, maybe, alcoholism!"

36
"Learn to be responsible
and accountable, always.
Pick up after yourself
and come up by your bootstraps.
A penny saved is a
penny earned, indeed.
Better yet, earn a dollar
and burn a dollar!
Think big, think outside
the box! Have faith
in our secular, military-industrial,
post-modern, political complex.

Thank you. Now, you may
proceed to your post!"

37
She walked into the spacious
front lobby. (Why, this is bigger than
the Bangalore airport lounge!)
The walls were lined
with shiny glass cabinets,
inside which were several
large sports trophies,
shining and very impressive.
The floor was also smooth
and shiny. Everywhere lay
large couches
and sofas, unoccupied.
"May I help you?" a voice said,
which turned out to be
a tall black man,
dressed like a cop, standing erect,
looking straight into Sheila's eyes.
(Why do they have to look so directly,
it's disconcerting!)

38
"I am Sheila Bhaskar. I am the new math
teacher."
"Oh yeah, they told me about you. What did
they say,
you from Korea, India, somewhere like that?"
"India," Sheila said helpfully,
at which Mr. Martin
(his name was embroidered
on his tunic) smiled,

suddenly becoming friendly.
"That's right. Come, I'll take you
to Mr. Moody's office.
I know he's expectin' you."

39
Led by Mr. Martin, Sheila
walks down the wide,
spacious hallway to
the office of Mr. Moody,
the school's principal.
(It's so quiet, classes
 must be going on.)
An older white woman wearing
glasses looks up at
Mr. Martin, who explains.
"Let me see if Mr. Moody
can see her now."
She goes in for a brief
moment, and comes back out
and advises Mr. Martin,
"She can go in."
Ms. Reynolds, who
studiously avoided
looking at Sheila,
sits down and resumes her job.
The job of looking bored—
not just bored—under-utilized,
and obviously pissed.

40
"Ah, come in, Ms. Bhaskar,
I hope I said it right!
Come in the house,

come on board.
Welcome to Martin Luther
King High School!"
Another big black man,
looking like a boxer,
dressed in a nicely pressed suit.
(I must say, some are so well
dressed, while others so
slovenly.)
Mr. Moody seemed friendly,
warm, and outgoing.
(But what is it, not very "refined?"
Sheila passed judgment,
feeling a trifle guilty.)
"So, you gonna help us
with math? Why, that's excellent!"

41
"You see, it's very hard
to find math teachers—good,
bad, or indifferent!
Everything else, they're
dime a dozen. Right now,
it's math teachers and
registered nurses. Both are
in great demand. I told
my daughter—she's in college,
studying Adult Ed.
I want her to major
in math, yep!"

42
When the two walk out,
the hallway is bustling

with kids between classes.
All are African American,
except for an occasional white.
All–boys *and* girls—Sheila noted,
were tall and big;
some bigger than
Mr. Moody, even Mr. Martin.
"How old are they?" Sheila asked.
"Well, let's see. Anywhere,
from fourteen to nineteen," Mr. Moody
replied,
as some kids made way for them
and smiled at the principal,
while others, who hardly noticed,
kept squeezing the gals
and talking to their pals.

43
Mr. Moody shook his head
helplessly and said
"I hope they aren't this rowdy,
back where you're from!"
Sheila politely smiled, conjuring
the contrast between
Hoysala Higher Secondary School,
and Mr. Moody's
Martin Luther King High School.

44
Mr. Moody conducted
Sheila around,
showing her the school
and the people therein.
"This here is the Guidance section.

Meet Ms. Rosser, and I'll
let *you* tell her your name!
Let's walk into
the Language Arts class.
Ms. McHenry—she has plenty
of smarts and class.
Oh, yeah, how can we
skip the library?
I mean to say, the Media Center,
that's what we call it.
We carry a lot of
entertainment videos,
which are real popular
with the kids."

45
"A truckload of computers
from the Gates Foundation
just arrived. We're still
trying to figure out
just what to do with'em.
Here's the auditorium,
which we just had refurbished.
We have a pretty decent
drama program,
a music choir, and a marching band.
Ms. Bhaskar, we've everything
except for a good
tenth-grade math teacher!"

Untrammelled America, No More

This segment begins with a lament over the stultifying effects of civilization's arrival on what was a pristine paradise. However, the poem readily concedes that "civilization happens, ready or not." The poem depicts the arrival of Europeans on American soil, beginning with Columbus, and their wilful conquest of the virgin North American continent and its native people.

46
The untrammelled America
was one humongous garden.
Verdant, vast, with a soil
which needed very little toil.
Anyone with eyes and a heart
could see it was
a celestial garden,
created by none other
than the one who
gave us the stars and the moon.
It was meant to be
a simple scheme.
You take your lover's hand
and walk in the garden,
discerning her happy face
by the dim starlight;
on radiant nights, you cover
her fine face with
yours, to protect her from
the glare of the full moon,

tinged with green. All kinds
of created creatures
crawled about contentedly.
A doe would stop to be
patted by the woman's
soft hands.
When the morning came,
it was no longer kindly
celestial light. The strong
sun's rays brought with them,
the short and impatient
shadows of civilization;
and plans to replace the garden,
from where to launch a walk
on the same munificent moon!

47
Civilization happens, ready or not;
in leaps and bounds,
over ages and eons;
dynamic, goal-directed, and
dramatic, at times;
subtle, subterranean, and
surreptitious at others.
Civilization is simply
a synonym for change.
A constant, continuing,
cumulative chant,
"Go forth, pick up the pace,
break it up over there!
For better or for worse,
there's gonna be a change.
Throw out the leftovers,
you sentimental fool,

change last night's sheets,
they're no longer cool!"
Who's doing it? Who needs
these new-fangled ways,
when we just had it right
and cruisin' along, thank you!
Not to be cute, but we're
all named in the lawsuit,
a class action on a cross-section
of the entire Creation!

48
They sailed from Cork to New York.
For some, it was Boston or bust.
From the banks of the Rhine,
they arrived in Northern Maine.
They set out from the familiar shores
of Britannia, for the coast
of sunny California.
Some covered the long distance
from the south of France!
Others, from Naples all the way
to the Vermont maples—
all entered through Ellis Island,
in the footsteps of the early settlers.
They colonized, occupied,
and tillaged the new earth,
foraged the forests of
a land of bounty
and unlimited scope.

49
America, the vast continent–
pure, pristine, and serene—

Lord knows for how long
it's been around or where
the First Peoples came from;
how they found their ways
of living in harmony
with the many creatures,
and Mother Earth's features.
Natural was their credo,
organic was their approach.
Spontaneous and instinctual,
they shared the land
with the mustang and buffalo,
until the day when the skies
turned dark with cumulonimbus.
And in sailed tall ships, steered
by Christopher Columbus.
The tired, hungry,
and near-dead mariners
were greeted by their Fellow Man,
with wondrous smiles
and open arms.
"Hello, Mr. Civilized Man! Welcome
to the land of the Noble Savage!"

50
Alas, Capt. Columbus
was in no mood for ceremony—
a conquistador, who lost
his way, and his cool.
"Where's the spices,
you dumb mices?
We've sailed across the world,
over uncharted oceans,
survived pestilence

and distilled essence;
seawater and seditious sailors;
and finally arrive
in the East Indies.
But this is a hollow victory,
very likely the snafu of the century!"

51
"Where's the gold? Where
the silks, cardamom,
and peppercorns?
Is this really the East Indies,
the land of tiger, elephant,
and the king cobra?
Isn't there a Rajah around,
holding his kingly court?
Oh, don't tell me
I am plain lost!
Where on earth am I?
And you people, who *are* you?

V&S go to the Movies!

Sheila and Vijay go to see a remake of *The Sound of Music*. Instead, they blunder into the wrong theater, which is showing a pornographic film. Sheila storms out and launches into a tirade over the many perceived social depravities in America that offend her. The poet urges the reader to be understanding of the early disillusionment felt by many newcomers in their sought-after destination.

52
Vijay and Sheila veer
from their routine,
to take in a movie
at the Multiplex-16.
A remake of The Sound of Music,
the song of Sheila's safe
childhood, back in
Bangalore's biblio bastion.
Julie Andrews, as the
guilt-ridden governess,
tending to the cultivated
captain's brood;
the songs, scenery,
high society,
and in the end,
Hitler's treachery;
what a film, what fantasy!
The apple of every Indian
moviegoer's eye!
Sheila hated the thought
of a remake,

yet couldn't resist
to go take a peek—
just to see how they
could tinker with something
so sacrosanct!

53
Vijay drives round and round,
until he finds a space
between a Miata and a Sonata.
Humming a Hindi tune,
he walks in with Sheila,
who, having had nothing
but the morning granola,
suggests they grab some lunch
at the Chinese place,
outside the Movieplex.
Coaxing in some noodles,
they wash it down
with veg drop soup.
Stuffing the cookies
into their pockets,
their fortunes on hold,
they rush into the foyer
and fumble in the dark,
looking for the right theatre.
"Was it 14 or 15? Why don't
they display the title?"
They decide it's 14, which
they enter on tippy-toe.

54
On the wide-screen
is a girl, not much over nineteen.
A natural blond, fit for a feller

like agent James Bond.
Her face flushed with
youthful vigor and excitement,
she's looking intently
at another young character
in blue jeans, long hair
and not much else.
Without warning, the girl lifts
her shirt, pulls it over her head
and removes it entirely,
revealing two fleshy,
milky globes pointed straight
at her lover! Sheila gasps in
shock, and sheer incredulity.
Is the woman mad,
to engage in
such crude vulgarity?!
Anyway, what has this to do
with her sweet *Sound of Music*?
Even if it did, she's nothing to do
with such brazen lewdity.

55
Sheila elbows her husband,
whose mouth is agape
at the bare beauty,
as he watches the
lucky young fellow
stoop ever lower,
and kiss the lass all over,
in full frontal nudity.
"What's this trash—I thought
we'd bought tickets
to *The Sound of Music?*"

Vijay shushes her and whispers
"after all, this is a latter-day sequel
to that sixties-old skitty.
Let's give it a few minutes,
to see where all this may fit in."
Sheila hangs her head,
avoiding the offending scene,
and begins to sob
not too surreptitiously,
making the other gawkers
turn, if only momentarily.

56
At which point, Vijay, nonplussed,
takes her hand, and they get up and walk out
of the salacious, skin-clawing flick.
Sheila is outraged; furious is not the word!
She drops Vijay's hand
and marches briskly, straight ahead!
He chases behind her,
feeling all mixed up.
It's too funny to cry,
yet too serious for laughter.
When they reach the Corolla,
Sheila straight gets in.
As Vijay cranks the engine,
it's plenty apparent,
his dear wife is distraughtened.
He drives the car, a somber,
chastised man, looking straight
through the windshield,
at nothing in particular.
Once they're home,
Sheila storms into the bedroom,

shutting the door behind her,
leaving poor Vijay
biting on his keys!

57
After a judicious delay
of seven minutes,
he ventures to go talk it over.
He opens the door,
and finds her lying across
the bed with one arm
draped over her eyes.
Vijay sits on the edge
of the box springs,
careful to muffle any squeak,
for it's a matter of life and death
for the rest of this
Great American Weekend!
He touches her elbow lightly—
still very still and inert.
He clears his throat
and bleats her name,
feeling much like a *halal* goat.
She flings out her arm
and turns to face him,
her face flushed
and red from the crying,
her hair wrinkled, in
disarray—but she looks
attractive! Weird.
You never can fathom women,
discern their moods,
nor gauge their reactions.
Why, this is proving to be

an entire course
in human relations!

58
"You want to know why
I am, well, pissed?
Because you're so
devious and complicated!
Why didn't you tell me
you wanted to go
see a dirty American movie?
You know, I don't care for
such trash! Yet, you tricked
me into going with you
in the name of my all-time
movie hit!" Inveighed thus
and chagrined, Vijay takes
a deep breath before copping
a defense. "My dear Sheila,
let me first apologize for
putting you through such
an awful experience.
I know you're no
different from my sisters,
or my mother, for that matter.
Your values are very high class,
and you care for nothing crass.
You're a chaste Indian woman
from the land of Brindavan!"

59
"So, what really happened was
a comedy of errors,
er, well, a tragedy, really.

We bought tickets
for Number Thirteen,
but we innocently
walked into Theater Fourteen.
No, it wasn't The Sound of Music,
or its sequel. What we
were watching was
The Dubuque Debutante Devils!
Only later did I notice
the ad, on the way out."
Mollified somewhat
by her mate's polite petitions,
but not quite over her
reactive revulsion, Sheila
gives vent to her
cross-cultural consternation.

41

Math Runs in Sheila's Blood

This segment traces Sheila's mathematical
heritage and academic preparation in India.
In the US, she faces the challenge of teaching
and motivating inner city American children.

60
Math runs in Sheila's blood,
counting one, two, three, four.
Her dad taught at
the University of Mysore,
and published numerous papers
on higher-order Gyrometrics.
His father, a proven math prodigy,
sailed to Oxford, playing
champion chess with shipmates.
Alas, in the end, it was his
beloved numbers, which did him in—
as eighty-nine plus three,
just couldn't be disproven!
Growing up in the long shadows
cast upon her, Sheila
fought the math mantle
that was rightly passed to her.
She identified more with her mother,
a vocal proponent of *Carnatic* music,
and focal point for the family fabric.
Sheila turned down entreaties
from several sought-after schools,
discounting tuition waivers
and assistantships.
She preferred to be like her mummy,
and sing musical praises

of Purandara and Thyagaraja,
while being a wife and mother
in blissful domesticity.

61
Had Fate not fetched
her a Math diploma
from the Hindu College
for Teachers,
Sheila wouldn't be
in the current dilemma,
standing in front of
this class at MLK High.
It's her first day of teaching
in the US of A,
a far cry from the crowded
classes of Hoysala High.
In a class of twenty-four,
eight were absent, she found out,
as she called the roll.
Names and name-calling
are proving to be her nemeses.
Ms. Prim and Proper, Sheila
felt competent, even confident,
in all areas except
the parsing of proper nouns.
Is it McDonaald or McDdonald?
Brux, even though
it's spelled Brooks?
For their part,
the Americans addressed her as
Ms. Bhaskaar, not Bhaaskar;
never mind the students,
who'd simply cover

their faces and giggle,
and not even attempt it!

62
There were six boys
and ten girls
in Sheila's Algebra II.
The ranks of the boys
thinned, once you get
past the 10th.
Mr. Moody talked about
the Tenth Grade Temptation,
when boys who haven't
already been claimed
by the street, would
simply give up
the pretense of school
and pull out altogether.
The remainder tended to be
fairly focused on graduation,
if not college.
So, Sheila felt fortunate
to have this bunch to coach,
and metric mysteries to teach.
They were quiet, seeming
attentive to her
pedagogic attempts.
They were big; they were black.
Many were handsome,
even stunning in their looks.
But all were clearly
in need of scholastic guidance.

63
A Mind is a Terrible
Thing to Waste,
so ran the slogan
writ in big letters
across the gym wall.
Does she have what
it takes, to lend a helping hand?
Does she have what it takes,
to mend a child's
modus operandus?
Sheila drove home pensive,
barely paying attention to
traffic intensive.

Chain Link Fences—Vijay's Domain

Vijay, new to prisons, cannot help but be impressed with the basic mission of incarceration, which is the security of the community, and how it stands in sharp contrast to that of a free society. He goes on to record his positive impressions of US prisons, which include a deliberately designed environment aimed at overall efficiency and an elaborate healthcare apparatus. The segment also includes the story of Crazy Black Joe, which typifies the struggles of many inner city black men.

64
In the land of Freedom, first and foremost,
where the outcry is:
"give me liberty or give me death,"
where the call of the bald eagle
heralds the free spirit,
what is more ironic
than iron gates and barbed wire,
which ensure, even
enshrine, captivity?
The chain link fences,
ribbon-like steel-sharp
razor wires, cut deeper
than flesh, bone, and
sinew, they puncture
the very heart and soul
of human aspiration!
Guard dogs and shock troops,

and fry-on-touch perimeter
defenses do more than
deter attempts at escape,
they leave one feeling
fearful, fatalistic, and
filled with deep despair.
Handcuffs, leg irons,
and sundry mechanical constraints,
serve to fetter more than
arm and limb;
they chafe at a man's pride,
and what's left of his dignity.

65
Who is hurting worse,
the brother or his keeper?
A question into which,
it may be worth
probing deeper.
The prison guard
mans the gate,
being an instrument of the state.
He seeks total control
of his quarry,
body and mind, if not his soul.
He clings to the comforting
illusion of a basic difference
between himself and the captive.
His uniform and trappings
serve to maintain distance
between himself and the convict,
as does his cultivated
sense of scornful disdain.
Little does he know

that the enclave
of suffering, however well
sealed and concealed,
has a way of seeping
into the community at large.

66
Madness it might be, but they
certainly have a method.
Vijay Bhaskar was quite impressed
("Exceeds expectations")
with the thought and organization
which went into running
this network of American prisons.
Thought and organization—
the twin qualities of which
the inmates were
inherently incapable.
If one could indeed assess
a society by taking a peek
at its penal institutions,
the USA should, at least,
get a Minus-A,
Vijay gratuitously graded.

67
These places are planned
for men to lead entire lives;
to hang their hats on a wall
and have a pot to pee in,
to put it plainly.
They are not mere jails,
which are way stations
before the Promised Life

behind bars. The prisons are
deliberately designed environments,
stark in their simplicity,
and minimalist to the max.
There's nothing disjointed
about these joints,
which have to deliver,
thrice a day, a hot meal tray.

68
Each body is kept warm
at exactly 98.6, and
provided basic accouterments,
to spend the unnatural Natural
Life, it was ordered to serve:
a cake of soap, a striped
prison-issue pajama,
a soiled *Playboy* pin-up,
a fading Polaroid print, and
a form letter from the Parole Board
guaranteeing yearly reviews,
until Kingdom Come;
the Kingdom Shall Come,
the gilded Gideon guaranteed.

69
Guaranteed also is access to
health care, a saving
grace of these hostile hostels,
provided at a great cost
to the taxpaying and ax-grinding
citizenry, passed grudgingly
by a divided General Assembly.
Vijay was mystified by

the minute attention to their bodies,
most prisoners seemed to pay.
They had the latest ailments,
to test the many panaceas,
and pharmacopoeias.
And given their long,
solitary days,
which afforded up-close
examinations of their bodies,
every pore, scar tissue,
every sniffle and sneeze
was reported up the ranks,
thanks to the Morning Sick Call.
TB is as persistent
as an incessant cough;
AIDS and HIV are part
of the inmate alphabet soup;
Herpes and Hepatitis
are commonplace hazards.
A sizeable number are
mentally encumbered: Depression,
Developmental Disabilities,
Borderline Personalities with
self-injurious proclivities,
Schizophrenia, Psychasthenia,
and Megalomania–a veritable
potpourri of
intrapsychic ailments.
Enter Dr. Vijay Bhaskar,
who has come all the way
from the land of *Pushkar.*

70
"Hi, how are you? I am Dr. Vijay Bhaskar.
You wanted to see me—

what seems to be the matter?"
"Well, I'm just feeling wretched,
like it's the first trimester!
I can't sleep, I can't eat,
and what I do,
I can't keep.
Like something heavy
is weighing me down.
Don't know what
to make of it.
Maybe you could make
some head or tail out of it?"

71
"Well, you will have to
tell me more
about your situation.
How much time
are you sanctioned?
What misdeeds
and *mea culpas* brought you here?
Tell me about your childhood
and neighborhood
in order to be fully understood."
"Alright, I feel you.
I'm Joe Blow,
known around the yard
as Crazy Black Joe.
I am doing
10 to 20—*years*—that is,
for chronic check forgery.
What it really was,
was courtroom treachery.
They made me cop a plea

and still shot me down
with the high trajectory!
You want me to go on?"

72
"Please go on, Mr. Blow," Vijay encouraged.
"Well, doctor, maybe you should
get you some coffee,
because it sure is
a long story, and, too bad,
I can't pay you no fee!
I'll spare you the distracting
details, because, believe me,
I know—cause I used to have the ADD!
Truth be told, I was born
to a crack mom and a dealer dude.
Dirt poor, for sure, we were,
which made things downright simple."

73
"What's for dinner was
what we had for supper!
But love and loving,
we had plenty of.
Mom's sweat
and the man's shoes—
human smells and cheap thrills.
When the dude left, moms wept,
but going we kept,
not knowing no difference."

74
"School bus came,
school bus went.

Sleep in with moms,
or watch the toons.
As the world turned,
it was one day at a time.
Good times on the tube,
bad times in the hood,
it's a life of
nickel and dimes.
Life's like the ocean—
you can't really swim;
just learn to float your
boat or life will
grab you by the throat!"

75
"Murky models and pie dogs' yodels,
a life of looting and shooting—
Heroin or high velocity,
whichever is handy!
For some, life is a lottery,
like a radio
with a dying battery.
It's hit-and-miss
for us black blokes—
you just hope the other
would miss!
You see, us poor folks
are life's real jokes."

A Blemish on World History

Dr. Vijay Bhaskar, the newly employed prison psychologist, asks his professional supervisor why there are so many African Americans incarcerated in US prisons. In response, Dr. Thayer refers back to the tragic course of history—that of America and most of the Western world. He also touches on the residual social effects. Back at home, Sheila, acting as Vijay's domestic guide, again puts things in perspective for her troubled husband and urges him not to concern himself with things they are powerless to change.

76
Vijay met Dr. Thayer,
Travis Thayer, Ph.D.,
in the central office.
An aging, experienced,
prison psychologist, Travis was
naturally genial and compassionate,
and very taken with Vijay.
Travis was instrumental
in Vijay's employment with
the Adult Corrections Department.
As the head of
Psychological Services
for the entire system,
Travis was Vijay's professional
supervisor and guide;
more, a mentor and well-wisher.
A rare American prototype—
cosmopolitan and

culturally comfortable—
one found them in
university departments,
and embassies
of the State Department.
77
"Hello, Vijay Bhaskar. Come in;
it's good to see you!"
Travis received Vijay warmly,
inquiring, "So, how are
they treating you?"
"Are you referring to
the inmates or the prison staff?"
was Vijay's sarcastic sally.
"True, I always found dealing
with the inmates, easier by far!"
Dr. Thayer smilingly conceded.
"In any case,
do you have cases
you care to bring up
this morning? Any that
stump you, discombobulate
or demoralize you?"

78
"Yes, to all of the above!
Although I've hardly
been here a few months,
I must say already
I have seen plenty.
I didn't bring specific cases
to present today.
But I have several impressions
I've been forming,

which need bouncing off
someone like you."
"Go ahead, Vijay—shoot!"
ordered the elder.
"First of all, I notice
there are a lot
more black inmates—African Americans,
I mean to say, than any other group.
What's your take on that?"
79
"Well, I knew you were going to
bring that up—it's fairly obvious.
I will say it has more
to do with sociology
rather than psychology.
And a good bit of history, I'm afraid.
Unfortunately, in every society,
it's the people on the margins
who're edged out:
the poor, the ignorant,
the incompetent, *even* the insane.
Darwin had it right—at every level,
it's the survival of the fittest,
including the human species."

80
"It takes a variety of skills,
traits, and attributes—
you'd probably add good karma—
to avoid the fate of incarceration.
As for the preponderance
of African Americans in the
ranks of today's prison inmates,
it's a complicated story.

"Their fabulous, well fabricated bodies of
ebony
were what attracted the greedy,
ghoulish traders who could
only see money.
The Innocents were bodily
lifted and brought out west,
thus starting a stressful chapter
in world history,
very likely it's very worst.
"A rather dark passage,
a dreadful documentary,
deeply scarred by pain and misery.
Why, the heavy bells of history
are still tolling in our
compelling, collective memory…

81
On the way home, tooling around
the traffic in his compact Corolla,
Vijay was reflecting on
Dr. Thayer's message.
A consummate professional,
Vijay felt lucky
to work under an American,
who is closest to a sage.
It wasn't what he said,
but how he said it:
with conviction and clarity.
But Vijay was well aware that
in the sorrowful saga of slavery,
America was but one chapter.
The shrouded, muted issue of
caste-related atrocities,
back home in his Hindu-India;

the unutterable practice
of the Untouchable—hastily dubbed
Harijans, or God's people
by Mahatma Gandhi;
their oppression by
high-caste Hindus,
perpetrated by
Vijay's own *Brahmin* brethren;
man, a social animal?
Just barely.

82
"*Saakappa, Saaku.* Enough.
I don't want to spend
too much time talking shop.
Besides, what can we do,
brand-new immigrants,
barely tolerated,
other than do our jobs
as sincerely as we can?
You're talking about
difficult, entrenched issues
that defy deft solutions.
Here, help me cook some
uppittu, darling. I've brought
some fresh bell peppers
and tender green scallions.
Cut some red onions
and a couple of potatoes,
please. Some ginger
and *mirchi,* as usual, honey.
Nothing like a whiff
of *Asofetida* in fresh hot oil,
after a long day of
superpower toil!" declared Sheila.

Arun Kumar, ABCD

V&S attend a party celebrating Arun's
graduation from high school. The poem
reflects the relative prosperity and success
attained by the Indian immigrant community
in America. The party helps V&S find another
couple with whom they can make friends.

83
"Dr. Kumar, actually, his wife,
Kaanchana, is asking us
to a party tomorrow night,
at their place.
It's their son's
high school graduation.
She says he'll be attending MIT!"
Sheila told Vijay,
who was checking his email.
Vijay went online,
to get directions to
the Indian Internist's reportedly
resplendent residence.
Sheila wore a smashing sari,
a cotton-silk affair
with Kanjeevaram *jari*.
She wore her hair
in a French braid,
and brought out her
wedding day jewelry,
smiling broadly at
Vijay's admiring glances.
He wore *Kurta-Pajama*,
and walked out in *Sholapuri* sandals,

to their first outing—
an Indian social gathering.

84
"Hello, *Namaskar*, please come in!
I am Kiran Kumar.
Kanchana's inside, eagerly
awaiting you!" A short,
balding man with a cherubic
face, Dr. Kumar moved with
ease, which came from a
carefully cultivated
bedside manner. A lovely
mansion at the end of a long,
private drive, into which
the guests started pouring in.
"Hello, I am so-and-so. So glad to
meet you! Have you recently
arrived? Well, then, you must
make it a point to visit us!"

85
Sheila was delighted to meet
so many Indians in one place.
She was awash with
a sense of security and safety.
Why, these were the pioneers,
many of whom have been here
three or four decades!
And successful beyond
anyone's dreams.
They were the doctors,
scientists, and professors,
businessmen, even a few

bureaucrats. A group that
counted among the wealthiest
of Americans. Yes, they're Americans,
no longer Indians—just think!

86
Many of the guests were
much older, who made
Vijay and Sheila feel
a warm welcome.
The elders still remembered
their faltering first months
in this complex confederation.
So, they took to the new couple
wide openly, recalling and
recognizing their own
now-fading faces,
in the young people.
There were other younger
couples present,
who, though perfunctorily polite,
were less welcoming.
They were quick to contest,
compare notes, and establish
turf and territory,
like straining terriers out
on an evening stroll. The food
was salivatingly
inviting and decadently
delicious. There was no
alcohol, but plenty of sodas
and fruit punch—a salute to
sweet tooth in
the sugary new land.

87
"Hi, I'm Nalini, this is my husband,
Suresh," said the young woman
in the turquoise sari,
greeting and smiling at Sheila.
Sheila smiled back and reciprocated.
Suresh and Vijay shook hands
and began to chat, leaving
the ladies to do likewise.
Turns out the new couple
are also from Bangalore,
having completed
one year in America.
They spoke in Kannada, switching
to English now and then,
a modern Indian habit.

88
The two couples stuck
to each other
for the rest of the party,
sensing security
and compatibility,
eager to solidify
acquaintance into
strong friendship.
Together they greeted
young Arun, the college-bound
son of the Kumars.

89
Arun had an entourage
of young friends,
many girls among them—

mostly Indian.
They all stood closely
together, away from
the others, busily chatting,
until it was time for cake cutting
and speechmaking.
Like many ABCD's,
Arun spoke with a
distinctly American accent,
rolling the R's, and
stressing and distressing
on the syllables self-consciously.

90
The audience was told
that it came down to MIT
and CalTech., and that
the East Coast won out.
"Our kids are doing very
well in America," observed
an elderly man who wore
a blue sports jacket, with a red
tie and white silk trousers.

Black History Month

Deals with the painful yet proud history of African Americans. Sheila finds herself in the middle of a social/political crossfire between those who sympathize with the difficult legacy of blacks and those on the other end of the political spectrum who hold more conservative views. The prevalent tension is proving to be too much for our math import!

91
It's Black History Month
at MLK Senior High.
Classes crashed to a halt,
and culture came to the fore.
The frowning, fault-finding
faculty betrayed
signs of softness
and sensitivity.
They became good sports,
and donned robes
of Mother Africa—
red, green, and yellow.
They took pains to
tell the students
"Always remember,
we built this America
with our blood, sweat,
and tears;
but never forget
you're really from Africa!
Remember too, the strength
of your forebears.

You have every reason
to feel proud, as any
Zulu warrior
who walked tall and
whose battle cries
were bloodcurdling!"

92
So well publicized
is Black History,
it's no longer a mystery.
Just a matter of outsourcing,
decided at the last Board Meeting.
Manufacturing needed human-
resourcing to bulk up
and buttress the homesteading
of freedom-loving heroes,
who just fought and won
their own independence.
It didn't occur to them, however,
that they couldn't turn
around and oppress other humans;
oppress, repress, and run
them into the ground,
like a rusting black Mustang,
driven till the engine
revved its last.

93
They don't lack for heroes,
for pain and strife
are the very soil
from whence emerge
real life De Neros—even

darker and handsomer.
Malcolm X, Martin Luther King,
W.E. Dubois, Booker T.
Washington, Thurgood Marshall,
we can keep on going.
Men who tackled problems
weighing a ton.
Accomplished athletes who
penetrated the popular psyche,
a raison d'etre for the
makers of Nike.
Versatile vocalists and
inspired instrumentalists,
enchanting to the ears,
and satisfying to the soul.

94
These earthy, colorful
chromatics were the perfect
antidote to the audacious
achromatics—the stoic and
severe settlers,
who were dour, with
a serious demeanor.
Sheila is clueless coming in to
this historical human drama,
still continuing
and carrying on,
with new players enacting
the arcane ethnorama.

95
"No, I am afraid
you have it all wrong,

Ms. Bhaskar—you've been
rubbing elbows with
the bleeding-heart liberals!"
opined Ms. Godwin, the white
Social Studies teacher.
They were talking over lunch,
in the Teachers Break Room.
Sheila was partaking
a *parotha*, stuffed with
potato and cauli,
while Ms. Godwin was
tackling a large bowl of chili.
96
"You ought to give us Republicans
a chance to tell you
what exactly is going on.
We're for racial equality,
Civil Rights, and all that stuff.
What we don't care for,
is all this crime,
teen mothers and grown
brothers' living off the dole.
I want them to pull
their load and not depend
on my tax dollar!"

97
"I'm not sure where
you're from—India or Irian Jaya?
It doesn't really matter.
And I don't know why
you left your country.
Is there some civil war
going on, or whatever?

All I can tell you
is that here we try to run
a country
which is fair to all.
And, if you work hard,
you can achieve
the American dream.
It's that simple!
We are a Christian country,
yet we let you practice
your faith, whatever
that might be.
Just pay your taxes,
and stand up and be counted.
We believe in family values
and old-fashioned worldviews."
98
Sheila, never one to
probe into
culture, politics, or history,
finds herself in the foreground
of a veritable social actuary.
People of different backgrounds,
ethnicity, and economic
self-sufficiency, sit around
the social round table,
ducking and dodging,
taking potshots,
trying to advance
their own group's cause.
The Haves against
the Have-Nots;
Religious Zealots against
Academic Atheists;

The Grey Panthers versus
The Youthful Upstarts.
"Ayyo, Ayyappa!" exclaimed
young Sheila,
as she hit the ground running
in her Secunderabad satin sandals.

Music Moves This Superpower!

Sheila, a classical vocalist trained in the South Indian *Carnatic* tradition, feels at home in America, a nation that is abuzz with music of all kinds.

99
Sunday morning saw Sheila
up, bright, and early.
It was high time she resumed
her singing practice.
"You're only as good as
how frequently you practice!"
was the sobering reminder
of her voice teacher and maestro,
Music Treasure–Muthu Swamy Iyer.
"I want you
to give concerts in America
and help spread our music,
when you get over there."
he exhorted Sheila.
She brought out the large *Veena*
from its cavernous case and
sat in the worship room.
She meditated for a minute,
before she strummed
the taut strings.
She plugged in the little box,
which supplied a
steady thrumming drone.
She began with *Vaataapi
Ganapatim Bhaje* in
raagam, Hamsa Dhwani.

Vijay woke up but stayed put,
enjoying the well-known *varnam*.

100
Sheila's sounds that morning
traveled far and wide,
into the land of music.
It's music that moves
this great nation;
music of all kinds,
more than even
ethnic cuisines—
after all, it's the food of love!
"You're from where?
Oh, the land of Ravi Shankar, okay!"
America's energy and vibrancy
is in its vast stores of music.
These otherwise mundane,
materialistic people, whether
campus kids or trucking types,
all come alive at shows
and concerts, or just listening
to their FM radios.
The Blues, Bluegrass, Pop,
Folk and Country;
Rock & Roll, Latino, and Reggae;
Dixieland Jazz, Techno,
and Dance Hall; the variety
is endless and
the beat goes on!

101
Musci makes this Superpower supple.
Without it, it'd be a cultural desert:
predictable, mechanical, and inert.

Music is what makes Johnny go!
Mozart, Bach, Beethoven,
Tchaikovsky, and Stravinsky
for its brain; Brother Charles,
and Lady Holiday, for its soul;
with umpteen other traditions
providing the chorus.
"Sheila, baby, you too bring
high credentials:
Thyagaraja, Purandara
Dasa et al. Yep, bring
on the old saints!
We hear you, we feel you,
we sure do!"

102
Rajni brought her daughter,
Uma, on a weekday after school,
as the 4th grader was keen
to learn vocal, *Carnatic* style.
Sheila smiled and welcomed
the visitors into the lamp-lit
living room, patting
the youngster's shoulder,
in aunt-like approbation.
Uma, slender and still tender,
smiled shyly, concealing
all emotion, pressing her
pad and pencil down
with her pretty, pointed chin.
"Today, we will begin
at the very beginning,
singing *sa-ri-ga-ma-pa!*"
coached Sheila, sitting on the floor.

V&S Attend an American Wedding

Vijay and Sheila attend the wedding of Tasha, Sheila's teaching assistant. In addition to poking satire on weddings, the segment also shows the Indian couple feeling culturally lost in the African American church celebration, bringing out the insecurities and petty prejudices of the visitors.

103
Sheila and Vijay attend
a wedding,
their first witness of such
an American proceeding.
It was possibly record-breaking;
for an East Indian
is rarely present
at an African American
nuptial gathering.
It was John & Tasha's
predestined day,
after many a tussle
saying yay and nay.
Tasha—light-skinned,
lithe and limber,
has been assisting
Sheila, since September.
A committed Christian,
caring but controlling;
without Tasha, Sheila
might be sitting at home,
playing the veena or viola!

104
Vijay followed Sheila,
who allowed her hand
to an escort,
who proudly marched them,
the youth's heart pounding,
at the brush with
the foreign queen.
The organ began spreading
the mood, calling in
the marriage muse,
settling down the pews.
"Dearly Beloved," began the priest
looking at the gathering,
before turning to look at the two,
who are taking the leap,
looking deprived of sleep;
still, they flash Colgate smiles,
looking regal and
resplendent, like
a right royal couple
from an interior African realm.

105
Subjected to sanctimonious,
soul-searching, sweatogenic
series of questions,
without one last option
to mull over the propositions;
confronted by
their closest kith and kin,
the couple, rather like bleating-sheep
on the sacrificial altar,
said the right things

and saved the day—
for themselves
and those congregated,
who heaved a sigh
of collective relief.
The parroting perpetrators
finally pressed lips,
on priestly command!

106
Vijay and Sheila remained
stuck to the pine,
watching John and Tasha
walk, their bodies entwined.
"It's called the Recessional,
so stay put!" chided
Sheila into Vijay's ear,
sharing the latest tidbit
of the fastidious,
foreign folkways.

107
All were later moved to
the church basement,
where they were duly seated.
With their brawny, black elbows
on the white-cloth tables, they
wait patiently, as
the bride and groom
snuck away
for their first photo shoot.
Sheila and Vijay,
sitting silently were
objects of curiosity,

being the only ones of
non-denominational,
non-African variety;
a cause for mild excitement
and passive speculation,
for the more-bored-
than-hungry horde.
For their part, Vijay and Sheila
staged prosocial smiles,
feeling a bit flustered,
though quietly accepted
by the dusky denizens
of The Other Side of Town.
Looking around, Vijay said
in a whisper: "These are
the faces behind the masks
of children you teach,
and the brethren I reach!"

108
At last, arrived the couple
with their perfumed party
of bridesmaids, best man
and the banjo player.
They spilled into the narrow hall,
humid with humans.
"Now, here come
Mr. & Mrs. John Sinclair!"
someone declared,
as Tasha and John headed
for the Head Table.
Vijay leaned over and
asked his wife, "Should we
go congratulate Tasha,

and be on our way?
I don't think they have anything
for a pair of veggie eaters
from Southern India!"
Sheila smiled her quick
agreement and got up
from the creaky metal chair.
They sneak their way out,
excusing and apologizing,
squeezing between rows.
They are all smiles, as they
greet Tasha first, and then
her brand-new John,
wishing them happiness
in their newly joined lives.
109
They walk out of the musty
marriage basement, feeling
like a submarine, which
broke out from underwater,
into fresh air and forgotten sunshine.
The streets are deserted,
as Vijay and Sheila walk
back to their Corolla.
They feel a sense of
accomplishment, at having
attended the exotic celebration,
and a silly sense of conspiracy,
at having eluded the
meaty, cheesy, white-breaded
cuisine. "Lord knows what
all they eat. Tasha warned me
of the so-called soul food.
I heard they eat pigs' feet

and other terrible meat!
Ayyo, Deva! If only my
Grandmother heard of all this!
Vijju, how are you and I
to cope in this carnivorous,
calorific, caterwauling culture?!"
said Sheila, nuzzling her
Corolla-coaxing, co-conspirator.

A Hopeless Night

A forlorn song about a prison execution.

110
"There's an Execution this Friday;
for this man who killed his
entire family—his wife and
the kids—but didn't kill hisself!"
hissed Secretary
Pam Parker, wheeling on her chair,
drinking weak coffee.
Vijay has seen the gas chamber
along with the others,
while on a tour of
Castlegate CC.
A stark little chamber
with two wooden chairs,
expressly installed for
a pair of treacherous twins,
who bade a joint goodbye—
for treason, the visitors were told.
There were other legends
of derring-do Dillingers,
who said their last prayers.

111
"I'm glad I am not required
to be present. I can't stand
the thought of such a cruel fate
diligently dispensed,
after due deliberation.
I'm not sure which is more
premeditated: the calculated
cunning of the contract-killer,

79

or the constitution-codified,
Common Law decapitation?"
"Nah, I ain't gonna lose
any sleep over it.
You see, doc, I hate to say this,
but the son-bitch should've
been gone a long time ago!
I do believe in eye-for-an-eye,
and tooth-for-a-tooth.
Even Steven—treat me
like you want to be treated.
You come after me with
a pointed barrel, I will blow
you away with a bazooka,
it's that simple!"
said Bill Simmons, the only
male secretary, noisily
chewing on a Double Barrel
Doublemint bubble gum.
Vijay looked down,
thinking, how come
he couldn't
think in black and white?
"Anyways, I'm just glad
I am not required to be present
just to watch the man
face his *karmic* comeuppance...
I am just glad I'll be
deep asleep, well
before the 2 AM deadline."

112
It was a hopeless night.
The air was still.
Still, the candles died.

The song subsided,
and the tears stopped.
The night grew darker,
longer and deeper,
when a mercy slumber
finally took over.
The entire group gathered
outside the walls—
lifers and pro-lifers—
lay lifeless,
as the real Lifers
within, too, slid into sleep,
allowing their cursed
comrade to quietly pass
into the long, dark,
and hopeless night.

Sheila's Challenge

This describes Sheila's attempts at teaching math to her 10th graders, who thrive on her positive attention and encouragement. The administrators and, at home, her husband recognize Sheila's special efforts.

113
"Boys and girls, you need to
calm down before you can
think and solve a math problem!
Otherwise, A plus B will
seem like A times B.
A quadratic equation
will appear to be
a trigonometric proposition!"
cautioned Ms. Bhaskar, smiling
benignly at her Tenth Grade class.
The pupils smiled back
and settled down,
responding to the foreign
lady's forthright ways,
knowing intuitively that
she wanted them to succeed,
go to college, and merge
into the Great American Middle Class.
A hand went up, a girl's,
calling for help.
"Yes, Latoya, how can
I help you?" Sheila asked,
walking over to the third row.
"Oh, very good, you've tackled
the tough part correctly.

Just follow through
with the remaining steps—
excellent!" she offered praise.

114
"The children like you, Ms. Bhaskar.
I heard many good things
about your class.
I'm sorry I didn't introduce myself.
I am Roxanna Roberson,
Curriculum Specialist!"
Sheila smiled and shook hands
with the tall and hardy
visitor from the District Office.
They looked at some
textbooks the specialist brought,
and discussed the merits
of some midterm measures.
That was when Sheila
decided to share an
idea, still threadbare,
with the well-connected
official from the
Superintendent's staff.
"I would like to train their
minds to think smart,
by playing chess and
solving puzzles, et cetera,
before I throw them
math problems
that seem menacing."
Sheila ventured.
"Why, that's an excellent idea—
I'm sure the kids would love it.

I will get you the materials
before the month's end."
promised Ms. Roberson.

115
"It's quite a challenge to train
a mind away from adolescent
American avocations,
and turn it towards
Teutonic tutorials and formidable
mathematical formalisms.
How to interrupt heedless
hormonal impulses,
which are socially reinforced
and naturally nuanced?
Inculcate interest in
matters of the mental realm,
which ought to be intrinsic?
Teach abstract, abstemious
algorithms, which seem so
inaccessible and impregnable?"
Sheila wondered out loud
in the presence of Vijay,
who was reading a book
on sexually deviant
serial killers.
He took her hand and
squeezed it, saying
"Perhaps you should approach it
as you would
teach a foreign language.
It's difficult, unnatural, and
forbidding, but basically
learnable and can be fun!"

Sheila, impressed with
Vijay's smart suggestion,
squeezed his hand back and
headed for the shower.

Prison Suits

A glimpse into the day-to-day operations of a
high-security prison and its administrators'
headaches.

116
Another Monday morning,
dreary and wet.
The Management Team, as per plan,
met in the Training Room
by the kitchen door.
The warden took charge and
brought to the fore,
burning issues
which needed urgent
attention, and those
that could do with a brief mention.
The agenda was sent out
in advance, listing areas
which they needed to
enhance, and items they
condemned as contraband.
The warden made it plain,
he wouldn't stand
irate inmates breaking
showerheads, nor grudge-bearing
guards cracking inmates' foreheads;
gory details of governing
a garrison full of men whom
no one claimed as their own.
The prison suits
bashed heads and stormed brains
till the morning's donuts
moved down their GI drains.

On the Edge of the Garden of Eden

This segment describes the hardships experienced by residents of the inner city. It starts with a soliloquy by Tasha, Sheila's teaching assistant, who laments the severely deprived lives of many of her tenth-grade pupils. The poem goes on to recognize the semi-heroic efforts made routinely by the elders in the community to step up and help where they can.

117
It's Tasha's task to take care
of the problems, many students
brought to school.
Tesheia's dad was sent to
prison, while Melanie's mom
messed with mescaline;
Rashad was caught with
a roll of weed,
whereas Alton was arrested
for concealing an Automatic;
Inner city children, insulated
from wonder and warmth
supplied routinely to
their suburban cohorts.
On some days, Sheila's sincere
assistant sits back and wonders:
"I don't quite know
what we're going to do,
about all these
daunting problems.

So many kids wanting
for things so basic, so
essential, there just isn't
a village which will do!"

118
Growing up in a government project,
like weeds poking through
a paved parking lot,
the children are left to
fend for themselves;
to grow up street smart,
but book-averse;
growing in spite of
their biological benefactors,
not because of planned
parental prescriptions.
They are the children of
children, who, seemingly big,
adult, and tall with manly muscle
and matronly manner,
are themselves
lost, lonely, and listless;
too busy in their own misery,
to tend to their progeny.
Together, they make a weed garden—
strong, tenacious, yet tetherless;
growing on dirt, wind, and rain,
on the very edges
of the Garden of Eden.

119
Don't get them wrong—they
won't have it any other way!

They're at home in
their part of town,
on their side of
the railroad track,
watching the freight cars
pass them by.
Heavy metal crushing
everything in its way,
carrying the sins and
social burdens of a
material society,
slowly losing touch
with its humanity.

120
"Southern Serves the South";
"Southern Gives Green Light
to Innovation!"; you can't
blame a railroad car,
nor its green and white slogans,
for failing to stop at
a promised station
and deliver the goods,
per designation.

121
But life goes on, no matter.
Babies are carried and
duly delivered in the
county health facility.
They're brought home
to the 'hood, where they belong;
joyously received,
by relatives and neighbors

who make a cake, and
cool lemonade.
The baby is smothered
with love and laughter,
and accommodated
in a crib, by the door.
He is brought up
by surrogate stand-ins,
as the mother
simply moves on.
No one complains,
but simply care for
the baby and his
big black teddy bear.

122
Once again, it's grandma to the rescue
of the growing little boy,
who needs a proper place.
She frees up a room,
and has it painted
a light shade of blue.
She squeezes her dollar, and
buys shirt and collar
for the latest little man
to come in her house.
The Lord giveth, and
the Lord taketh.
She's seen it all in
her seventy-odd years.
You learn to show up
and do what's right,
leaving the rest to the
government and the Good Lord.

"You're comin' up on two,
still, your daddy hasn't showed.
What're we gonna do, big guy?
Your mom is gone, and
daddy is Lord knows where!
But we're gonna find a way—
we always do.
Praise be to the Lord Jesus,
the everlasting and merciful!"

Immigrantitis–Vijay's Serious Seminar

This lengthy and serious segment deals with immigrant psychology—the crux of this drama. Suresh and Nalini are joined at home by their friends, Vijay and Sheila, all of whom take turns venting their pet peeves and personal observations, with reference to their newly adopted land and culture. In the end, it falls to Vijay, the psychologist in the group, to put it all in perspective. He does this by coining the term Immigrantitis, which refers to the various phases in the cultural adjustment immigrants undergo, allowing them to assimilate gradually, after initial resistance and confusion.

123
"Hi, Nalini, hello, Suresh!"
said Sheila and Vijay, walking in.
"*Banni, banni, kooth koli*,
come in; please have a seat."
welcomed Suresh, leading
them into the formal
living room. Both pairs
were genuinely pleased
to finally find a
compatible couple,
with whom to speak
their hearts out
in their twisted native tongue,
compare notes, and
complain stoutly.

Nalini led Sheila
into the *Puja* Room,
where she had a display
of the devas and deities.
Into the bedroom, next,
to her collection of silk saris.
The two young women—it was like
they went back to a time
in their childhood,
playing, sharing,
and just hangin' out.

124
Suresh is a techie,
a de-facto designation
for today's Indian young men.
He worked long and
hard for Microsoft,
using skills and codes
to solve their nagging
business problems,
bringing the binary code
to benefit someone
else's bottom line.
It's a clean-cut line
of work. No sweat beads
nor soiled hands,
as long as you had
an A+ in C++,
and a Camry car,
to carry you far.
But a techie is nothing
without his ThinkPad,
like a junkie
without his juje pejes.

Just park him in
front of a monitor,
hand him a mocha java,
programmed for
once, on the hour!

125
"So, how do you like your teaching job?
I heard it's difficult to
teach the American kids."
asked Nalini, nursing her
V-8 juice. Sheila replied
"yeah, it's quite challenging
to teach in the city—they're
quite underprepared—
you wonder what they've
been doing in the early grades.
Poor things, most of the kids
are from needy families.
Some are orphans,
and destitute.
Very sad, but many live
in violent
neighborhoods—it's a
wonder they even
come to school.
Unlike back home,
here, they have
a law for compulsory
attendance. So they arrive
on the school bus alright,
but no more motivated
to learn than
Vijay's prison guys!"

126
"They're all so big and tall,
you wouldn't believe
they're teens, at all!
They dress, it seems,
to attract attention.
Especially the girls,
who aren't overly
modest. They seem
preoccupied by sexuality,
and yet, so young they are!
Of course, as a fellow
South Indian, you do
understand: this place—
I don't know—most things
seem skin-deep;
They preach faith and
family values, unless these
include heedless hedonism,
and instant gratification;
I hate to be so judgemental but
there's no stress on
sense and sensibility, and
seriousness of purpose!"
Nalini just nodded,
as she is just getting
to know Sheila and
not knowing what to say.
Things are very different, true,
but so seems Sheila Bhaskar,
that much is apparent!

127
"Sheila, dear, your impressions

are aligned exactly with mine.
But, as a psychotherapist,
I am also having to
learn a lot; a lot about
the codified
cultural mores
and preferred practices
prevalent here.
You and I both are having to
undergo nothing less than
a cultural reeducation!
As you know, at work,
I have first-hand contact
with American people.
I talk with my patients
and read their family histories.
I chat with colleagues
and my other American friends.
So sad, people get into
so many problems needlessly, it seems.
As a psychologist, I cannot be a moralist.
I cannot ask the obvious:
why can't they refrain
from actions which are
guaranteed to garner
nothing but grief?
Neither can I preach, saying,
let children be children,
and learn their ropes
from caring and protective
parents. Nor can I ask
adults to model
sober, sanctified, and
sophisticated ways.

Because that would be
asking too much
in this land of personal
freedom and I-me-mine liberty."

128
"Oh, the ladies are solving
the world's problems!
Who started on such
a sober subject?
I bet it's our Nalini."
said Suresh, squeezing his
pretty wife's strong shoulders.
"Sheila, here, is no less
opinionated. If it's left to her,
she would straighten out
all social problems
in a summary fashion!"
chimed in Vijay.

129
The women smiled at each other,
and looked at
their young partners.
Suresh went first, saying
"why get into the crevices
and crannies
of this zany society?
They're made differently;
they *think* differently.
If they hear your suggested
ways, they will brand
you a grandma, as they'll
find your views insipid,
and your values, quite vapid."

130
"They've built this nation grand,
these children from the Euroland.
They've explored all possible
avenues and left no stone
unturned, endeavoring
endlessly to make their
lives comfortable
and contemporary.
In the process, they've
overstepped natural constraints
on body, mind, and soul;
oversupplied and overfed
every whim and fancy,
every surface and orifice,
innocent and impervious
to our time-tested mantras
of moderation and modesty,
safety, sanctity, and sagacity!"

131
They all turned and looked at Vijay,
who was listening intently,
leaning against the living room wall.
"I hate playing the psychologist
when away from the couch.
Yet, I can't help but observe
that we as immigrants are going
through what I call Immigrantitis.
I mean, new people arrive
here daily, in this, the land of
their hot dreams, only to
wake up in the morning
to face cold realities.

The newcomers find
the place to be too big,
too complex; its people,
rather smug.
It's like, "Here I'm in
America, but the picture
isn't quite right..."
They look around and
see America, with all
aspects unveiled.
Everything is magnified
to the bug-eyed visitor.
The good is very good,
even awe-inspiring, while
the bad is repulsive;
thanks to the media graphics."

132
"The new arrival can't
quite arrive at confirmed
conclusions. He goes through
phases, as his stay increases.
At first, his ambivalence
is in ascendance,
as he feels threatened
by the disparity in
sheer size between
continental America,
and his Lapland,
the Lesser Antilles,
or wherever he happens
to be from!
He defends his dictatorship,
and derides this free-floating

ship, but only till he finds his
deck, and gets over sea legs.
He's now grumbling less,
and even gambling on his
chances of advancement
in the opportune land.
No longer a vagabond,
he settles down with
the grimy Green Card
firmly in hand.
He then makes it his business
to stem the flow of foreigners
into his newly adopted land!
At long last, when he finds
his Brave New World
no longer new, nor so brave,
'let's go to the polls' he bellows,
'and throw out the old rascals!'

133
For some, it's as if
they have arrived at Heaven's Door!
'Meritorious Members Only'
the freshly painted sign reads.
Posted: 'Those with good
deeds, degrees and
pedigrees only!'
'Oh, you've got the
Pearly Gate Passport, golly!
And the verified, vaunted visa?
Very good, this way please!'
But, even a heaven
needs getting used to—
until the earthly spells and

one's mother's cooking smells wear off.
So it is with these
United States of Aspirations!
You scramble to get here,
and tremble before Peter,
the INS Inspector,
who lets you in
duly disembarking at you.
Your visa is adjusted,
your very life, readjusted.
Over the years and decades,
you're transmogrified
into another affluent,
arrogant, all-business American!"

134
"*Eno*, Vijju, you have turned this
into a serious seminar!
BS, it may be, but
sounds very impressive!"
teased Sheila, secretly surprised
at her mate's astute
assessments.
"But seriously, honey, you are right.
I should learn to not be
so judgemental, and
begin to accept this culture
as it is, and appreciate its context.
I will try and do
just that, thank you!"
Sheila vowed aloud sincerely.
"That's right,
Vijay. Indeed, it's impressive
how you're able to analyze

this America attraction;
or, is it America ambivalence?
Whichever, it reminds us to be
mindful when we're
around you, the fact being
you're a trained psychologist!"
added Suresh, who's
more at home with
dealing with machines,
than nations and their machinations.
"I don't know about you all,
but all this heavy-duty
discussion has made me hungry.
Oota thayyaride—lunch is ready.
Let's see, we have *uppittu,*
vobbattu and *oothappa*.
And, of course, *bisi-bele-baath*
and *happla*. For an added
American touch, we've cool
pralines-in-cream
for dessert!" narrated Nalini.

Doctor From the East Counsels Inmate From the West

Vijay employs notions from Eastern philosophies to help prison inmates deal with very difficult personal problems.

135
He walked in with hands
cuffed behind him,
two escorts walking in his wake.
Vijay motioned him to
the only chair in the room,
a green plastic one,
on which bold red letters
spelled INMATE, which,
in reality, spelled doom.
The fellow was in his
late twenties, a white man with a
wiry build, his head
clean-shaven. He peered
at the psychologist
through icy-blue eyes in
which Vijay saw
brightness, even mischief.
"So, you're the psychologist
from India, I've been
hearing so much about.
The guys tell me you're into
meditation, the Buddha,
and all that cool stuff!"
Vijay smiled, reciprocating
the cool vibe.

136
"Let's see, what's on your mind today?"
Vijay began the doctor-patient
privileged conversation.
"Oh, just a few things, really.
Stale things;
the same old thoughts
keep making the rounds,
like the merry-go-round mustangs
at the county fair.
These thoughts—they're
like my children—though I would
just as soon disown them!
They're mocking little
bastards, who make me
feel bad and have me
quaking quietly."
"What are these thoughts
about, Mr. Waddell,
that so plague you?"
"I have got AIDS, you might
have heard. No, not from no
homo, but a shared needle!
I also have pending
charges in New Mexico—they
say I killed a tribal chief,
outside an Indian casino."

137
"You do have big problems,
Mr. Waddel. Very real,
and not imagined;
they are eating away
at your T-cells, and

scouring your very soul.
You can give in to anxiety
and other allied neuroses,
or tweak your mental messages
such that you rise above
the idle thoughts, like
late afternoon clouds
which go up to meet cool
breezes and bring on rain.
So, go ahead, Mr. Waddell,
sob and shed your
condensation. You're
just a product of your
Prarabdha, not a whit
more, not a bit less."

138
"Call me a frail-minded fatalist,
or an easy spirit from
the lazy East! With all
due respect, I submit
that there are some problems
which are best left alone
and given a rest. Yes,
your folks have walked
on the moon, and currently
working on walking on
water! You're excellent
at conquering the
external elements.
You forecast foul weather,
run-down rapid winds.
You combat cancer and
discover distant stars.

But when it comes to
matters of the heart,
or issues that make you
reach for the tissue, trendy
technology wouldn't do,
not even tricky therapies.
Instead, you look within,
face the truth,
and come to terms."

139
"No use flailing against
things which are *fait accompli*.
If you have AIDS,
or that you have murdered a man,
gruesome as they are, they're
in your past; liable to
ripple into the present,
only if you let them.
You are just a sum
of your past actions;
you can look at a man
and see that.
You can tell the kind
of life he's had,
some of which is his
doing, and the rest was
thrust upon him.
The fact that many prisoners
are born into poor homes,
were raised by incompetent,
ill-equipped indigents,
is two strikes against them.
It's then left up to them

to destroy themselves,
at a pace and place of their choosing!"

140
"One could counter such
a depressing, deterministic
view with examples of
lotuses that bloom out
of mud or perfect duds
coming out of brightly lit
homes. However, those
are the exceptions, which
prove the rule. I'm afraid
the computerists had it right.
Garbage in means garbage out!
But how's one to cope
with such a cold reality?
First of all, you recognize
coping is all one could do.
Get yourself to look at
yourself—no use denying,
devaluing or discounting
the problem. "For whatever
reasons, I've engaged
in actions that fetched me
AIDS—it's real, like
this rash on my arm!"
Secondly, mourn the fact
that it's a deplorable
state of affairs.
Shed a tear and do
lick your wounds.
Finally, realize that
there's more to you

than living the life
of a wretched AIDS patient;
that you're part of
a bigger spiritual scheme
in which AIDS is just a blemish."

141
"Sure, it's easier said than done.
It calls for persistent practice,
constant reflection and
course correction.
It's a game played by
your mind against itself;
one side is trying to
pull you down,
while the other is
asserting its will.
Meditation will elevate
you above the fray.
It'll take you to that
place where Nothingness
reigns supreme;
where there is no AIDS, no prison.
Nothing good, nothing bad.
Just nothing, period.
Make a monastery out
of your prison cell, Mr. Waddell!
Mental mastery is much
better than passive misery!"

The Shiva-Vishnu Temple

Describes a temple visit that allows the Indian couple to remain in touch with their traditional rituals of worship, even though they are thousands of miles removed from their native country. They stop at an Indian restaurant for a heavy lunch on the way back and go home fulfilled in every respect. The satirical poem highlights the odd juxtaposition of the ancient culture of India, set against the commercial and modern backdrop of "Main Street, USA."

142
The Shiva-Vishnu Temple
sits on a prominent pimple,
overlooking the First Citizens Bank,
whose customers, pure and simple,
go unaware of
the exalted deities
installed inside the temple.
Lord *Vishnu*, in smooth,
milky-white marble–
sweet, benevolent, evoking piety.
Shiva, not so charitable,
dark and hard
in scarred black granite,
can end this
sense-existence
in a cataclysm,
with just a blink
of his third eye!
This point-counterpoint

of ancient Eastern mysticism,
is affirmed daily
by the charged cry
"*Hari-Hara Mahadev,*
Shambho Shankara!"

143
They walk into the temple,
sans sandals, their feet
feeling sandy.
Sheila reverently
hands the bundle
containing coconut, camphor,
and rock candy
to the waiting priest,
clad barely and smiling
austerely.
Vijay rings the big bronze bell
thrice, rather loudly.
The swarthy priest
blows the conch shell,
and utters *Vedic* chants
in stylized, ancient Sanskrit.
"*Om, Keshavaya Namaha,*
Shivaya Namaha,
Madhavaya Namaha!
Glory to Keshav, Shiv and Madhav!"
Keep us adrift while we're
lost in the ocean of *Samsara.*"
The worship over, they pay
for priestly chores,
and move about, gazing
at the zillion ancillary idols,
all-too-aware that

they're all from
one and the same source.

144
Thus sanctified,
they leave the shrine
and steer the car homeward.
On the way,
they stop at the Light of India
to join the monstrous
midday buffet,
greedily surging forward
towards pots of *idli, vadai, sambar*
and homemade ginger *chutney*.
They eat the condiments
to their hearts' content,
not caring to look backward,
until their tummies
bloat like Santa's
at the Thanksgiving
picnic-parade!
Seeing their distress
from carrying the weight of India,
the ever-vigilant Vimla,
wife of the proprietor,
tactfully clears her throat
and offers them bottles
of ice-cold Coca-Cola.
Thus revived, they burp
in gratitude, pay their
gratuity and walk toward
the parking tunnel, chewing
morosely on seeds of roasted fennel.

The Song of a Correctional Officer

The segment recognizes the secluded nature of prison work and the difficult/complicated role assumed by men and women Correctional Officers, who work in there. The typically isolated and remote physical setting of most correctional centers is inherently not conducive to easy media access. By the same token, publicity or due recognition for the admirable and noble service of the prison staff is also restricted. Officer Maggerty gives us his take on the subject.

145
"I was a Navy man—
I do know about
stealth and silent service.
Here's my salute to fellow sailors!
Now I am out of the water,
doing silent work of
a different kind—working in prisons—
which are tucked away
in the countryside,
away from public view.
A lot goes on in a prison,
each and everyday,
where men and women
render service that
makes for a long day!
The prison is a place
for confrontations
and contradictions.

As officers, our job
is to keep fellow humans
securely inside,
when they would rather
be out and about,
jaywalking, roadside!

146
"Someone has to do
the dirty work; it fell upon me
to keep 'em in line, and
maintain minimum order
in this rowdy crowd,
spoiling for a riot" explained
Officer Mark Maggerty.
"You've got to ride the herd,
yet keep 'em from running,
so they stay within the
confines of this
correctional corral!
No, I am no mean S.O.B,
like they would have you believe.
I'm just here to do a job,
I sure intend to.
I was taught to work hard,
believe in the Lord,
and respect the law.
I just can't stand by
and watch
a bunch of thugs
and sorry slackers
sit around sashaying,
sucking from us taxpayers!"

147
"You need institutions
of all kinds
to run an organized society,"
Maggerty continued,
"and people who get up daily,
get in their cars,
to go translate their
nightly dreams
into prosocial,
profitable pastimes.
You need schools, factory tools,
hospitals and health spas,
corporations and chambers
of commerce to help
decent dreamers self-actualize.
Yet, in every society,
there is a segment
of lazy, listless layabouts
who sleep during the day,
and go realize their
diurnal dreams
in the quiet of the night,
by the light of half-moon.
It's for them, they invented the
gated and corrugated institution!"

Sheila's Dream

Sheila experiences a nightmare that dredges up stuff from her childhood. Her husband and psychologist-bedmate, Vijay, readily and conveniently analyzes the dream, explaining "the true significance."

148
One night, Sheila had a dream.
No, nothing to do with
her hopes and her future
here in America.
One which took her back
to her roots, where
she was conceived
and constituted—on
the banks of the Kaaveri,
a place called Kalpakam.
She was a girl of four, dressed
in a shiny white satin frock,
walking into a wedding hall
along with her mother,
where a hundred people thronged
around the prettified pavilion.
Little Sheila joined some
cousins at play.
They all ran out into the street,
tumbling forward,
like freight cars on
the Guntakal to Gudur
goods train!
That's when a large black dog
appeared from nowhere,

and began to glare and snarl
at Sheila menacingly,
making her petrified
and paralyzed.
Someone—can't quite
tell who—grabbed her by
her arm and moved her
away from harm,
thank goodness!

149
Vijay grabbed Sheila's arm,
and roused her out
of the nightmare.
She was glad to see
her loving husband
holding her, on
their American-size
satin-sheeted bed.
"What was it, honey?
You're making these
gagging sounds.
Must have been a bad
dream!" Vijay guessed.
"Oh, God, yes. This big dog,
all black, with his fangs bared,
staring straight at me!
Apparently, I was at
someone's wedding.
I was, like, 3 or 4.
You know
how such dreams are—
there's no head or tail.
People and places are

all mixed up.
Anyway, I'm simply glad
it was just a dream,
although it seemed
all too real!"

150
"Here, drink some water
and gather your nerve.
Nightmares are not
the nicest things.
They have many theories
and treatises on dreams,
but I will spare you those
at this unnatural hour.
Suffice it to say most
dreams are products of
the semi-conscious self;
remnants from the
relegated realm, which go
unprocessed by the
wakeful mind. I couldn't
help but note the black dog,
and the white silk outfit,
which seem to symbolize
the refractory racial
realities that surround us.
But that's just a clinical guess!
In any case, good night, my
lovely woman...You've
really nothing to fear!"

Uncle Sam's Club

This humorous, satirical segment depicts the time-honored and orchestrated process by which immigrants assimilate into "the ethnic amalgamation called America," and how they eventually achieve individual psychological identities as Americans, all admittedly nebulous concepts.

151
This really is not one nation,
but an amalgamation
of many cultures, mores,
and mindsets, all melted
down to form the lowest
common American
denomination.
It's a manufacturing
process, a la Adam Smith.
You bring in your bona fides,
and back up your claims.
You're then dubbed
a Resident Alien—
an awkward designation,
to be sure, which leaves
you in doubt—"Am I in
or out?!" You carry the
Green Card, to the envy
of other American
wannabes, for a
five-year minimum,
during which time
you put in odd hours

at bad jobs and earn cash
to the possible maximum.
Whereupon they tease you
with a citizen's quiz:
on rights, freedoms,
and familiar facts,
having made sure
you speak their language,
think their thoughts and
pledge your allegiance.
Only then are you granted
membership to the
biggest warehouse store
there is—Uncle Sam's Club!"

152
Once you're a member of
this exclusive club,
you're invariably and
instantly indoctrinated.
What's the best ism of all?
Capitalism,
careful—with a capital C!
And the worst?
Communism—just look
at'em, Soviets!
What's the most just form
of government?
Democracy, definitely yes!
What's your fondest hope
for your son?
That he grow up to become the President,
is there a doubt?!
Which are the twin pillars

of a community? Policemen and
Volunteer Firemen—yes, sirree!
Which is the mightiest river
in the country?
The majestic Mississippi, mind you!
Name three quintessentially
American avocations?
Of course, Baseball, Apple Pie,
and Chevrolet!
153
This newly found Americanism
is further reinforced,
best of all, by the buying power
at-once accorded by
the almighty American dollar,
so, wherever you go, you can
throw your weight around!
Keep in mind that
there are all types of
dollars out there:
American, Australian, even
shiny Singporean imitations,
not to mention those from our
Nice Neighbors to the North,
who suffer daily humiliation,
when their dollar is
made to look smaller.

154
Our newly minted U.S. citizen
gets ready to board
the returning Boeing, saying
"back home for a few weeks,
we're going!"

It is a scene enacted daily
at all the major airports:
dragging, not an overnight
but an overweight American
tourister: a compact camera
slung over the shoulder
of his rakish Tommy T-shirt;
the prized American Passport
to legitimize and leave no
doubt of the American Express
checks bulging from our traveler;
not to leave out
the fresh-mint smell
of the twenty Twenties, tucked
away inside his tweed jacket!

The Peripatetic Police Pet

A humorous tale of police dogs brought into
prison to search inmates for contraband
items.

155
The guys were up early,
that morning in Seg.,
their post-breakfast siesta
interrupted by three eager,
duty-minded German
Shepherds pacing the halls
and wagging their tails.
Joe Blow stood at his cell door,
watching this unusual sight.
Canines among felons, chasing
them down as if they were
the hated felines.

156
This was an entirely
new dimension—the deliberate
introduction of
animals into the prison fray.
Joe has heard of the
notorious K-9 units
employed in evidence seeking
drug busts. 'But this here dog
bustin' into my prison cell,
why, this feels downright weird!'
"Hey, dog! I know you've got
a job to do, but
do remember, you're
still a man's best friend!"

157
The peripatetic police pet
quickly went through
Joe's 12x10, slathering saliva,
and scratching the floor.
She sniffed and sniffed while
Joe stood outside, feeling
miffed. She lingered a moment
in front of Joe's prison-issue
boots but came right out, nodding
at Joe, like 'I give you
a clean chit!' The handler,
a tall, husky man with
blond hair and a Prussian air,
glanced briefly at Joe,
conveying no particular
feeling and followed in
the footsteps of his
master-for-the-moment.
Joe reoccupied his rathole,
feeling a sense of reprieve.
He snuck his fingers between
the soles and pulled out
the dog-gone weed!

The Case of Becker Bartley

The tragic story involving a young man who was charged with murdering his mother and siblings while they were asleep.

158
There's the case of Becker Bartley,
despicable as it was dastardly.
He murdered his mother
and two younger sibs,
while they were
asleep in the middle
of the night,
in the middle of the
family double wide.
He was barely twenty,
a quiet youngman,
a self-avowed recluse
and video watcher;
now very calm and
unaffected by that
very recent night.
It's all still so fresh,
their *praana* is still traveling.
Clean-cut, all-American,
and well mannered
which Bartley was,
Vijay could discuss
everything with him,
except for the main question,
why. 'Why did you dispatch
them out of this world?'
Because, Bartley was yet to be
properly arraigned,

his culpability still
to be nailed down.

159
There he sits in his
yellow jumpsuit,
with no airplane
nor parachute in sight
to bail him out—out of
this unfathomable,
unforgivable, original sin.
He's just finished eating
his scrambled eggs,
washing down scrambled
thoughts with orange juice.
No thoughts, no feelings;
banish bothersome memories;
Be here, right now,
be in the moment, he strategized.

160
The black female prison guard
walked past his door,
her bulky posterior following
obediently behind her.
The guy next door
is hollering for toilet paper.
Someone on the PA System
calling a Code Yellow,
while the new fellow
on the upper tier is
asking for a softer pillow;
don't look ahead, don't look back,
just sit and focus on your breath...

A Town & Gown Collaboration

Sheila ventures to contact the local university
to have their students from the university
chess club come down and teach the game to
pupils in her tenth-grade math class. The
collegian volunteers arrive and teach the
cerebral game to the receptive high
schoolers. Sheila is pleased with herself and
"falls in love with life, with America!"

161
Sheila got in touch
with the local university;
a highly ranked private school,
heralded as the South's Harvard.
The Dean of Student Affairs,
to Sheila's great surprise,
deigned to look personally
into Sheila's rare request—
to have some stalwarts
from the university chess club,
go downtown to the
beleaguered backwaters
of MLK High School;
a Town & Gown coup,
to the Dean's diplomatic delight!
On the appointed day,
Sheila received them in the lobby,
and led the four checkerbockers,
two girls, two boys, all Caucasian,
into the cafeteria, which was
empty at this hour, where
the sugar and salt shakers

were filled to the brim;
next to which were the
checkered boards of chess,
with the pawns pleading
pathetically, "Please, push us around!"
162
Gary and Gail, along with
Abigail and Aaron were introduced
to Sheila's class, which was standing by.
Rashad and Raeford, Tihana and Teneisha,
were asked to come forward—
the opening pawns in
Sheila's strategic game.
They sat at the four tables,
set up for the mentor-mentee pairs.

163
There were many smiles and
giggles all around,
from the puzzled players
and curious spectators,
as the cerebral, cool,
and comical collegians
introduced the game, not
as a matter of grey matter,
rather as a challenge and
one-upmanship, based
on one-on-one cool—an
ultimate test of one's
capacity for chilling.
The kids walked around
the tables, watching
their playa-friends,
who're so mesmerized

they didn't mind
all the milling.

164
Sheila entered her
newly acquired Accord,
feeling ambivalent
towards the pungent, plasticky smells.
She carefully steered it
out of the near-empty
parking lot.
She's feeling happy,
even a sense of excitement,
at her academic experiments.
It's a sense Sheila's never
had before, never having
experienced it as a child.
It was an adult kind
of feeling, a sense of fulfillment
and soaring self-esteem.
It left her feeling
determined
to work even harder
for her 10th-grade class.
Stopping the Honda
at the grocery store,
she walked in humming a *filmi* tune.
She bought a frozen veggie pizza
with plum tomatoes and fresh basil.
Sheila drove home, falling
in love with America,
with life, period.

The Fall of Manhattan

Recalls the still traumatic terrorist attacks of 9-11 and America's reactions to the shocking scenes. This segment also focuses on the basic political identity of this proud nation.

165
Vijay's been watching CNN,
the 24x7 news channel:
news, politics, opinion
by talking heads going
yak-yak-yak, the average
American's TV turnoff.
But ever since the misguided
Middle Eastern militants
brought back Pearl Harbor
to the shallow waters of
the New York harbor,
the war-on-terrorism,
altered not just the
urban apple's landscape,
but the entire national
pastimes of escape.
The simultaneous ratings war,
waged via remote
control showed how
the happy-go-lucky nation
was unduly interrupted
by ominous emergency
broadcasts. Even the
commercials went off
the air, as planes
disappeared in mid-flight.

166
Enough has been said about
that waning summer day,
or has it?
Vijay, new in the country,
and new at his prison job,
was undergoing New Employee
Orientation that morning.
He joined the others
as they rushed
to the adjoining Break Room
to watch the surreal
conflagration unfold.
There was palpable shock,
as no one talked
but passively looked on
at the sooty images
on the prison's TV monitor.

167
Most in the huddled group
were too young to
remember Pearl Harbor,
besides being preoccupied
with their Nine-to-Five
to look beyond
everyday's borders.
Vijay himself didn't know
what to make of this,
though familiar with the
mindset of malcontents.
He walked to a phone
and called the school.
A recorded message crackled,

"due to unforeseen
developments, all
classes are canceled."

168
There's a grim and serious
air that season, even though
the smoke had cleared somewhat.
The usual festive features
and the Yankee Doodle
bands were fewer
and more muted,
as the nation was deadlocked
like a Manhattan gridlock,
over the two sparring
candidates. The Gallup Poll
hadn't budged—it's
a 50-50 dead heat;
no one could be nudged,
no swing voters nor
soccer moms, not
that election year.

169
Vijay watched with fascination
at the American political procession,
while Sheila kept busy
in the kitchen.
Here is a robust
and vibrant democracy,
arriving at bare
minimum plurality.
All attention is on
the candidates, as a

hundred cameras and
even more reporters
scour their past for
all kinds of antecedents;
everything goes in
love, and political war.

170
In a country bursting
with pride of their nation,
and its institutions, no one
occupies a greater pride
of place, than their most
beloved Mr. President.
It's a preeminent
position, acknowledged
as such by the
Congress and Constitution—
he's Da Man, Big Cheese,
and Head Honcho!
There's all kinds of glamour
out there—you've Hollywood,
the Fine Arts, and even
the Nobel Notaries.
But none can equal the sheer
power, pomp, and circumstance,
and the very presence of this
virtual prince, they lovingly
refer to as The President!
He can walk on water,
and leap over tall buildings—
"there ain't nothing,
the Prez can't do!"
so the loyal subjects sing.

MLK Chess Club

Sheila's move to introduce chess to her class by using student volunteers from a reputed local university proves a great success. Feeling encouraged, she then visits the Dean/Head of Mathematics at the university, seeking further assistance from the smart undergraduates.

171
The chess games charmed
the children such that
they founded their own
M.L. King Chess Club.
Mr. Moody was so pleased
he further seduced the kids
with pepperoni-on-pizza.
The simple move by Sheila
paid unforeseen dividends.
The college kids who felt
intrinsically rewarded
for their altruistic actions,
spread the word on MLK
across their wide campus.
Calls poured in from other
eager volunteers;
some students offered math tutorials,
while those into journalism,
wished to do a video on the
downtrodden children and
their uplifting teacher!

172
"*Howdene, eshtu chennagide ninna kelsa*!
Wow, Sheila, how nicely your
job is coming along!"
exclaimed Vijay, feeling
a tinge of envy.
Sheila just finished sharing
with him, her phone line
forays into the nearby campus,
yet to set foot
on the hallowed grounds.
"How smart are these
people, Vijju. I mean these
young fellows from the
university, which they
amusingly refer to
'as their school',
and fittingly wear shorts,
as if they still
attend Grammar School!
Anyway, the big news is
that Dean Broadhead,
from the Math Department,
invited me over. He also
wants me to attend their
Summer Teacher Institute."

173
Barry Broadhead was indeed
the Department Head of Mathematics,
a distinguished professor and
leader in the field.
Sheila was quite intimidated,
understandably, dear reader;

to go from the moribund
and modest MLK High,
to the privileged playgrounds
for pampered pates!
And, once there, to meet
with the main *Muni* himself!
She parked her Accord
next to a big fat Ford and
walked up the stone steps
to Hadley Hall. Aaron,
who was waiting, smilingly
received Sheila and conducted
her to the warren of
high offices, inside.
She was received warmly
by the distinguished Dean, who
quite looked the part—an avuncular,
Cronkite-like, affable figure.

174
"So, which part of India
are you from,
and how long have you
been here?" inquired the Dean,
rolling his chair back,
away from his desk;
he was very attentive
and extremely engaged.
"Oh, you're from the South?
Yes, I've been to
Bangalore once, years ago.
They had a conference
at the Indian Institute
of Science. Oh, yeah;
a very fine group of people—

I still keep up with their journals.
I've also been to Calcutta
on another trip, but I clearly
preferred Bangalore, I must admit!"
he said, with a mischievous air.
Reminded of her grandfather,
even her own father, to some extent,
Sheila shared her genealogy,
acquainting the Dean
with the areas of math in which
her forebears had flourished.

175
"Oh, is that so? But that's hardly
a surprise. You Indians have been
math fiends since day number one!
The great Srinivasa Ramanujan,
was a man of high renown.
You mentioned
your father's work
in the area of Gyrometrics.
There is one in our group,
who is similarly inclined.
Perhaps he's aware of
your dad's doings. In any case,
let's talk about *your* work.
I hear you're teaching
disadvantaged children,
trying to give them a leg-up.
Well, I am all for it, needless to say."

176
"Some of the seniors and
grad students have expressed
interest in assisting you.

Would you have any use
for tutorial help?"
offered the dedicated Dean,
clearly above the mean
in kindness. Deeply touched,
Sheila gushed, "I feel very obliged
to this university and your students.
You've already helped my class
quite a bit, but it would indeed
give us a boost if some of
your students came to provide
tutorial help. It's a fairly small class,
and they have given me
an assistant who's very helpful
in dealing with the children's
social problems."
"Very well, Ms. Bhaskar,
we will send a few your way.
By the way, you may
also want to attend
our Teacher Institute, over
the summer. It's meant to aid
situations exactly like yours!"

Dee Dee Dickerson

Sheila is made aware of the ethnic factor in public schools. She is encouraged to get out of her classroom during the lunch hour and eat and socialize with the others in the Teachers Lounge, where she meets Dee Dee, a young black woman, a friendly and hardy soul.

177
It's a quarter till twelve,
by the Principal's clock.
The setting: Teachers Lounge,
a lousy refuge from the crazy
centrifuge of classes.
Sheila rarely goes, so rare
that Victoria Verwoerd,
the white Vice Principal,
noticed and notified the novice:
"You shouldn't avoid the
other teachers, lest they should
misunderstand.
As it is, you aren't black enough,
whereas, in my case, I am
too white and wicked!
There's no winning with
these 'Minority Madames of the
American Public Academe!'
True, you're doing great work,
wreaking weekly miracles,
which is precisely what irks
these trade union oracles!"

178
"Hi, aren't you the new math teacher?
I'm Dee Dee Dickerson,
9th Grade Social Studies,"
she said, extending a friendly hand.
Sheila was grateful for
this solitary, social gesture.
So she sat next to Ms. Dee Dee,
opened her yellow
lunch box, and brought out
the plastic spoon with which
to feed herself mushy
Masuranna and Mango pickle.
D.D. looked and asked
"what's it that you're eating?"

179
Sheila felt embarrassed,
but somehow translated
the contents.
"Wow, I bet that's good...
I never ate any foreign food,
I didn't even try.
I did have yogurt ice cream
once, but I'd rather eat
the real thing! Where are
you from? India?
Does that make you Muslim?
Oh, I am sorry. You're Hindu!
I should've known—we did
Major Religions in the
Fall. Little Santosh,
he is Hindu—his mom
made some gooey sweets

for the class. I forgot
what she called them—
but they were *good*!"
Sheila's now trained to share
her ethnic antecedents,
and recite recipes to these
restaurant-reared raptors,
realizing that every one of them
was from somewhere else.
And many sought the recipe,
just to show respect for the other's
culture, not for cooking
that night's supper supplement!
Sheila, in turn, never posed
such questions herself
to her interlocutors from
a striking lack of idle curiosity.

180
It turned out Ms. Dee Dee
transferred in from
another high school,
the year before.
"That was an Alternate
High School, you know
what that is? Let me tell
you, honey. This ain't nothing
compared to what they have
over there. I mean, them boys
are real rowdy! They brought
guns; they even shot'em
on school property!
Lord, have mercy!
My boyfriend wouldn't rest

until I shipped out of there!
Whew-yee!" Ms. Dee Dee let out.
Sheila was quite amused,
and took a liking to Dee Dee
and her colorful diction.
Here was a woman,
who came up from tough
circumstances, yet leading
a successful life.
How impressive, what hardy souls?!

A Carnatic Recital

Another poem that stresses the cultural
freedoms enjoyed by today's immigrants to
the US. The short segment describes Sheila's
continued commitment to practicing classical
Indian music. She gives a recital in the
cultural hall of the temple on the occasion of
a religious festival. Vijay feels proud of her
musical talent.

181
Sheila was asked to give
a *Carnatic* recital
at the *Ram Navami* festival,
held at the Shiva-Vishnu temple.
Nalini and Suresh were
the joint emcee team,
being that both enjoyed
the gift of gab,
were fair of skin and carried
minimal flab. Sheila's solo
item was kept for the last,
coming on the tender heels of
many a children's dances.
They managed to arrange
for a trainee *tablaist*,
in the absence of a *Mridangam*
Narasingam from music-mad Madras.
Valli, wife of Mr. Vadi Velu,
had to do on the violin,
while the undertraining Uma,
was allowed to deliver the drone.

182
Vijay sat in the second row,
and watched his wife on stage.
Sheila shimmered in
her silken gold sari,
under the bright lights of the
Annamayya auditorium.
Sitting in the middle, allowing
the accompanists to warm up,
Sheila cleared her throat
and began to sing.
As per plan, she began with
Baala Gopaala in *Bhairavi raagam,*
set to *aadi thaalam*.
The complex musical aesthetics,
blended intricately with
the utterly humble sense of
Bhakti, which the lyrics
conveyed, were enough
to transport Vijay and
the others in the hall,
to the purest place
within each. Vijay has
never heard his wife
sing with the full orchestra
before. He found it thrilling,
and fulfilling.
The *raagam-taanam- pallavi* routine
was quite appealing as
the violin and percussion
joined in, adding to
audience delight.
"I'm so fortunate to have
married this mathematical
nightingale" exulted
Veeragandham Vijay Bhaskar.

Contest With a Skunk

The rantings of a frustrated prison inmate who is given to cutting himself just to get the authorities to pay attention to his needs. Desperation can lead to perverse thinking, making inmate Gales daring the authorities to a contest of wills, in which he is identifying with the repugnant creature.

183
"You don't get into a pissing
contest with a skunk,
haven't you heard?!"
reprimanded Guilford Gales,
inmate, addressing the
dreaded District
Classification Committee.
Gales was an inveterate
cutter, quick with the
razor blade. He cuts up
his own flesh in exchange
for the administrators'
fleeting attention.
The Time: 9:30 A.M.
Place: The CCC SuperSeg Unit.
Scene: Gales railing helplessly
at the prison officials gathered
for the half-yearly rigmarole.
"You sorry—oh, I'm sorry, I
see y'all brought a lady
with you this time—you folks,
you are all pressed-up and
powdered. They probably fed

you donuts and drinks
from the kitchen—hey, I
wouldn't touch 'em myself,
but that's on you!
You come to check on
us low lives if and when
it occurs to you,
like a fat, happy farmer
on a visit to the pigsty."

184
"And you wonder why
I cut on myself. Honestly,
if I have half a chance,
I will cut on the others—
the staff *and* my sorry comrades!
I do it because I don't see
any other way
to get these folks to do
what the state pays 'em
to do! We ask for the least
little things, like a roll
of toilet tissue or a pathetic
little postage stamp;
but no one helps you; they
don't seem to care or
give a damn! We can fill
out all the grievances we
want, but it's just a lot of
BS paperwork which ends up
in the trash. You can jack me up,
and put me in the dog house
each time I slash myself.
But hey, what do I have

to lose? Like I said,
you don't get into
a pissing contest with a skunk!"

185
"You tell me, what do I
have to lose?!
They done took everything
I ever had, not like I had
much to begin with!
You take a cat and back it
up to a corner—don't act
surprised if he sprang up
and pried your eyes out!
You might say I got myself
jammed up, in here.
Sure, it ain't no one else's fault.
Had I left that bottle alone,
and been faithful to my woman,
you know what, we wouldn't
be here conversatin'!
Still and all, the judge
sentenced me to fourteen
years in prison, period.
Not for no psychological torture,
not so the state can
play all kinds of *head games*!"

Many Americas Out There...

Vijay, a 24x7 "nonstop psychologist," reflects on the range and complexity of the American socioeconomic stratification. He concludes that "education, ethnicity and earning power" seem to form the brick walls that separate the different groups, even though all of them go by the label of Americans.

186
Vijay Bhaskar, the South Indian
psychology doctor is
standing at cross-cultural
crossroads, wondering how
to get a handle on the
complex American social
scene. To a casual, alien
interloper, "they all look big,
blond, and white" and seem to
carry the same few names:
Jim, John, and Joe.
"It's all about the whites,
and The Majority Culture;
the rest of it is simply
background-color and
clutter," Vijay concluded.
Behind the seemingly
class-free society, there's
clear socioeconomic
stratification. Education,
earning power and ethnicity,
appear to be the three E's,
that endure and form

the brick walls which
separate the people's
American experience:
where they live, what they
eat, and the kind of deal
they get. There are many
Americas out there,
insulated from each other
like the Israelites,
from the Intifadists.

187
Are you in a gated castle,
a make-believe private world,
with too much snazzle?
Do you, instead, make bed
at a county shelter, or, worse,
in a department-run dated castle?!
There are a thousand
in-betweens, and alternate
arrangements in this land of
opportunities and endless
options. Are you a middle-income
misanthrope, mincing
matters minutely, balancing
checkbooks cheerlessly?!
Or, the lucky one
who can just flash your
golden credit card
or scan the platinum plan,
so the gate lifts,
the peon salutes,
as the waters miraculously
make way?!

In any event, not to worry,
my dear fellow North American,
the worst of us will be
counted as middle class
members in most other chambers!
Take this, too, to heart: it's a
finite number of nights
before you leave this planet,
so, go now and
enjoy the good night!

Math by Way of Mozart

Sheila and her teaching assistant Tasha, take a moment to review the progress made by the class in response to the special teaching efforts made by the two of them.
Tasha is full of praise for Sheila, who feels grateful and takes the opportunity to unveil another innovation: the teaching of music to stimulate mathematical thinking in her students. She goes on to arrange an afternoon of music as part of her new initiative.

188
The Midterms were mercifully over.
MLK is eerily quiet,
as the kids are on
Christmas Break.
Sheila and Tasha are having
a relaxed, optional workday.
None of the others are around—
no finicky fellow teachers nor
bothersome bosses.
The two were savoring
a rare moment, munching
on blueberry muffins.
"So, half the year is over,
are we any further than
where we were?"
Sheila asked, like
a pilot to the navigator.
"Oh, most definitely, Sheila.
This here class is the most

motivated I've seen
in many a year!" Tasha replied.

189
"It used to be a job and a half
 just to bring'em to class
and keep'em focused!
We never had a whole class
to score at the 80th percentile!
The girls are doing better,
much better than the guys,
I'm afraid to say!
Sherika and Samantha
are striding straight ahead!
So are Leila and Latoya.
These girls just love you to
death, Ms. Bhaskar.
Be careful what you tell'em,
'cause they might just do that!
Why is that? I wonder
about it—I even go home and
discuss with John. Sure, you're
a fine teacher who knows her stuff.
And you've been innovative,
what with the chess games
and smart chats, et cetera.
But beneath it all, I suspect
the kids seem to know
you're their first-ever
teacher, even if a foreigner,
who cares and believes
in them to get it right!"
was Tasha's sentiment sown,
salutatorian-like summation.

190
Sheila, touched,
a trifle embarrassed, replied:
"Thank you, Tasha. I couldn't
have done it without your help
and support. I'm pleased
to see the girls are thriving.
I can see Sherika heading to
an Ivy League school—
she's fiercely focused!
You may have noticed,
it is the guys who have
taken up chess seriously.
Myshaun has made friends with
the men from the college,
and moving in the
right direction. His classwork
has picked up, as I was
hoping—a side effect of
success in chess, I just know.
Sylvester is smiling
more often, and submitting
his homework on time!"

191
"I have one more
card up my sleeve,
aimed directly at the boys.
They say math and music
go together. That certainly
has been true in my own case.
I talked to the newly hired teacher,
who is into instrumental jazz.
Mario's mom was a soprano,

singing with the great gospel groups.
And Jimmy's dad was
a jazz pianist before
he went to prison.
Music pulses in your veins
as lustily as
the great Nile
laps on its banks.
Let's work to awaken
the music-math connection!"

192
Sheila sought the Administration's
permission to introduce
Indian *Carnatic* music.
They set aside
the afternoon hours,
for the exotic recital in
the school's auditorium.
Sheila's conscripted class,
along with a few interested
faculty, including the new
music teacher, Brother Yusef,
sat quietly in anticipation.
Sheila tuned the strings
of the *Veena* and played a *raga*,
after explaining the alien
musical system to the small,
accommodating audience.
She then went on to sing
a long *alaap* for an evening *raga*,
which left the listeners—
young and old—mesmerized.

193
Sheila's musical initiative
was well received and
roundly applauded.
Next, Brother Yusef
went on stage and sat at the piano.
He played a melodious medley,
before inviting young Jimmy from
Sheila's class to take over.
Jimmy walked up shyly and
sat down before the Baby Grand;
Jimmy, to whom nothing ever
came easy except for music.
It flowed full and fluid
from Jimmy's fingers, or
was it from his soul?
That he was calling on
his imprisoned father,
the others didn't know.

194
"Boys and girls, thank you
for your patience and patron.
Music and the arts
are the very basis
for man's meaningful existence.
Without the arts, we are reduced to
robots, programmed into
a rut of a routine—
without thinking, without feeling,
doing, God knows, whose bidding?
Besides, musical practice every day
saves your faculties from decay;
your attention and concentration

will be A-OK. So, jump into
the fray and pick up an
instrument, starting today.
Math by way of Mozart,
is the modern way!"

Education is the Way Out!

College volunteers enter Sheila's math class and assist the tenth graders—"fresh fecund brains for fostering young minds..." The poem goes on to recognize education as the passport out of inner city exile and into the American mainstream.

195
Tasha divided the class
into three groups
and handed them over
to the college tutors.
Sheila had the volunteers
undergo a day's orientation,
sharing the curriculum
and her chief concerns.
She had them observe
the Algebra II class.
The volunteers, a quiet,
studious bunch—two males,
and a female—added a new
element to the small
huddled class: more energy
and vitality which the
two regulars couldn't quite
generate on their own.
Fresh, fecund brains for
fostering young minds.

196
Education is the only way out
of interminable, inner city

exigency. A four year college
degree covers up visible scars
of victimized pedigree.
Schooling lifts you
out of poverty, even if
years after you've
been done dirty. Sorry.
There's gold in the Federal
Fort Knox, but not for
anyone who simply knocks.
You've to pull out
your credentials and come
up with the collaterals.

197
Haven't you heard,
there's no free lunch
in this competitive,
capitalistic cafeteria?
Get a head start, overcome
your innate ADD, and
hit the *books*, not teachers!
Push back peer pressure
and stick with the Big Brother,
so, one day you put
on the cool cap and hood,
and dodge the neighborhood, for good!

Dr. Anand's Orations on America and Americans

In this engaging and thought provoking segment, Dr. Anand, an Indian immigrant who is a professor of anthropology, and who happens to be a cousin of Sheila, directs unabashed praise on and recognition of white Americans and their accomplishments. He describes the early challenges the European arrivals had to face while establishing their settlements, and goes on to zero-in on their unwavering work ethic, penchant for pragmatism, etc. The hands-on, practical approach of the whites, Professor Anand theorizes, is emblematic of their identity and is their most unique characteristic.

198
"Fright supremacy has morphed into
quiet supremacy,"
pontificated Prof. Anand,
Sheila's visiting second cousin,
and untenured Assistant Professor
of Anthropology at NYU.
"America unleashed the pent up
energies of the erstwhile
Europeans, who got out
of their tiny, stiff lipped
and lock-stepped countries.
The large spacious vistas,
and the rich, compliant soil
of the new virgin land,
evoked ideas that matched its
grand scale and proportion."

199
"The Euros, Anglos, Settlers,
however one referred to
them, the whites
were up to the challenge.
They thought big, more
importantly, they worked hard,
and threw in whatever it
took, much of which
was removing obstacles to
committed goals, whether
natural features blocking
their way, or hostile
human forces, which had no
clue about the new arrivals
with whom they couldn't see
eye to painted eye!"

200
"Persist they did, as only
white people could.
That might be their motto,
"persistence and present tense,
never speak in the past tense!"
"It was quite like a *Yagna* or
Yaaga our India's mythologies
describe. The Euros pulled together
against a common enemy,
and worked towards
a common goal.
Heroes were born daily
during the conquest,
and went down in the
early lore of this brand-new,

'straight-from-the-crate' continent.
They gave it a name and
made it their own.
Whether might is right,
it won the fight."

201
"The white guys simply
knew they were right,
that they were
the superior peoples.
Besides, who was there
to doubt or dispute!
Take any field of endeavor,
they're in the driver's seat—
the rest of us simply ride
in the crew cab, watching
the milestones pass, lazing,
taking in the scenery."

202
"They believe in endeavor;
wherever, doing whatever!
They're turned on by
doing things. They're like,
'Don't just sit there—*do* something!'
Pick up something, look it over.
Remove the screws, take a peek.
It needs a new part?
Go get it from Parts Central.
Does it work now? Check it out.
The green light comes on? Good!
No? Then, chuck it!
Get a new one—Malmart carries 'em,

or look in the Yellow Pages.
Don't let things go to pot,
nor allow things to rot
on your watch.
You and your toolbox
are going to heaven, aren't cha?!"

203
"How did they get to be this way?
The attenuated academic
answer is modeling and
managed expectations.
As an American, *doing*
is what you do!
Growing up, you watch others
do stuff. You try your
little hand at this and that.
Daddy will get Junior
a socket set and Navy blue
coveralls, for Christmas.
You're hardly a man
if you aren't handy,
one is told."

204
"The world is there to plainly see.
What you see is how it is!
Now, get out there and change it—
work on it, and *improve* it.
Leave behind a better America,
than the one you found.
Laziness is a sickness,
worse, it's a sin!
You don't want to be

shiftless and sorry;
You're doing the Lord's work;
take pride in it.
Take care of the
Red, White, and Blue.
Don't let the colors fade—
go get a can of paint!"

205
Anand paused for breath,
before resuming.
"Don't get me wrong;
I'm no knee-jerk singer
of Yankee Doodle praises.
But on balance, the USA
wins the most medals
in the Olympics
of overt material existence.
The rest of us can
stand by and watch the Stars
and Stripes rise, and listen to
their Star Spangled Banner
replay all day.
What's behind American success?
I believe it's their pragmatic pulse.
They don't see the world,
say as us Indies do.
The picture they see
is in need of repair
or improvement,
if not wholesale replacement.
For these guys, the world
consists of only physical
objects, which include people!

Americans spend their entire lives,
working on things and
working out things;
doing things to things,
and people!
They have to be able to
touch and feel with their hands;
otherwise, they lose interest!
One could say the Americans
are the most realistic lot;
rarely romantic nor idealistic,
even if they so insist;
they will quickly analyze
and break down
even those soulful sentiments
into the underlying, ugly realities,
just so they can then work on them!
'Give me the problem, gimme the specs;
I'll give you a ballpark figure.'
is the unequivocal American anthem!"

206
"Don't fool around, just tell me
what's wrong and we'll fix it!
If it exists, we'll fix it.
If not, call us when you have
a real problem.
Is something leaking, or broke?
Ain't doin' what it's supposed to?
Oh, you just want to go for a walk
in the moonlight? Why, we'll
let you go for a walk on *the moon*,
how 'bout that?!"

The Entity Called Effulgence

Dr. Travis Thayer, an experienced prison
psychologist, sheds light on the darker region
of human emotions.

207
"Emotional extremes are
inevitable, though rare.
Take sadism, for instance,
which certainly qualifies.
Thankfully, it's rarer than
its more ornery cousin,
garden variety meanness."
(Monthly supervision
for Vijay, from his Guru, and Guiding
Beacon: Dr. Travis Thayer, seated
in his black leather-chair, behind
which hung The Madonna and Child.)
"These are negative
but uniquely human traits,
no getting around it.
Take your Bengal tiger, for instance:
it's cruel by nature,
but never mean or sadistic.
The tiger can't go about
its business without being cruel,
just as a cow can't help being
a cow—docile and pastoral.
Isn't it why your people
designate it as holy?
For us humans, sadism and such,
are on the darker end
of the band of emotions;

while the positive attributes
of hope, optimism, and
a sense of wonder
lie on the brighter end."

208
"Why sadism, this degrading,
seemingly counter-human emotion?
May I propose my construct of
the effulgent human spirit?
Isn't it comical how our fellow
psychologists shy away from
the idea of spirit? It's like a
physician avoiding to deal with
the concept of blood!
The human spirit is the most
delicate and critical aspect
of the developing individual.
It needs to be fed and nurtured
by other mature and robust spirits,
in order to attain its
potential state of effulgence."

209
"When the spirit is healthy and bright,
one is the most hearty.
If the spirit is starved or, worse,
actively damaged by other
supposedly human models,
the result is a shattered spirit;
a den for untoward and
perverse traits, such as sadism,
meanness, and bullying.
All of us have all these qualities,
positive and negative, within us.

Which is salient and which is dormant,
which is fleeting and which is enduring,
depends on what's being
reinforced in one's environment."

210
"When one gives into sadistic
impulses, I suspect he's on a
slippery slope to self-degradation.
As abominable as his actions
are towards others,
they do not compare
to the severe self-loathing
he has to endure!
Sadism is preceded by
self-mockery, a feeling
that there's nothing
redeeming about oneself.
The person sees himself
as being ugly and utterly worthless.
It must be the most
aversive state, which
renders one lonely,
removed from the human
fraternity. It's in such
a dark state that the
individual turns on
other perceived sinners
and punishes them in
a perverse form of
self-flagellation by proxy!"

211
"It's depressing, don't you find,
even discussing it?"

remarked the obviously effulgent
spirit of Dr. Thayer.
"Let's now explore how we may
repair such a sad state of affairs.
Presented with sadistic and
cruel behavior, the society
typically makes a childish
response: we inflict
punishment on the offenders,
just to appease our collective outrage.
The wise thing, it seems to me,
would be for someone like you
or I, to sit down with the
person, without prejudice
and with all due respect,
facilitate a gradual
rapprochement between
the man and his lost
flock of injured feelings;
help him come back into
his own and the human fold,
by calling on our own
magnanimity and the entity
called effulgence!"

Smells and Sounds of Love

On a lazy Sunday morning, Sheila enjoys a
reverie which takes her back to her childhood
in India and memories of her mother's
cooking.

212
Sunday mornings are
Sheila's payback
for the public pedagogy
she practices all week.
She gets up early and
eats toast, this one day
of which she wants to
make the most.
She adjourns to the
living room and grabs
the Remote, lying uncontested
on the coffee-stained table.
Flipping channels, she settles
on a frumptious-looking
food-maker whose beefy hands
are amazingly nimble—
cutting, dicing and stirring;
chopping, mashing, and kneading,
all the while expertly yakking.
Meat, cheese, and wine, notes
Sheila; vinegar and Tartar sauce;
"God knows what all he's mixing!"

213
Sheila's thoughts travel back in time,
back to when she was

still in *langa and choli.*
She used to help her mother
wash the vegetables, string
the beans, peel potatoes,
and clean the rice.
Shobha Murthy was
a consummate cook,
who would move around
the kitchen like a painter
of murals, putting a dab here,
blotting a spot there,
seeming mindful and
in full control. Sheila loved
watching her mother
move about the kitchen
as if on autopilot,
from task to practiced task,
humming all the while in
Punnaaga Varaali, in pure bliss.
With such smells and
sounds of love are
some childhoods blessed.

Mindless Mollycoddling

The tale of a cynical and crusty prison guard,
who has a dim view of the efficacy of
psychological treatment, but who ends up
pouring out his own personal troubles to
Vijay, the prison psychologist, who comforts
him.

214
"I don't know what they call it
back in your country;
in this here county,
we call it mollycoddling."
sneered Officer Ladderman,
a scrawny, grey-haired man in
his late 50's. "I see you talking
to these inmates. I suppose
you call it counselin'.
Whatever it is, it's
a sheer waste of time.
Let's be honest.
These are hardcore
men, set in their ways;
there's no redemption for them,
they will so tell you!"

215
"Spare the rod and spoil the child"
you've probably heard.
These were spoiled rotten
and ill-begotten children,
who were allowed to have
their way and free to play.
I can't see them tell you

their sorry stories,
and play you for everything
they can get. Pardon me for
saying this out loud;
just a bit of
Harper county horse sense,
take no offense!"

216
"No offense, Mr. Ladderman.
I'm glad you spoke your mind.
I agree with your assessments,
matter of fact.
Many inmates do wallow
in self-pity. They grew up
without direction or discipline.
You have kids, don't you?
I bet they walk the-straight-
and-narrow!" said Vijay, disarmingly.
Mr. Ladderman put down
the heavy metal restraints
he was carrying and
wiped his brow, before saying
"well, the girls, they turned out fine..."

217
"But my sons...it's a different
story. Growin' up, I didn't
cut'em any slack. If they
acted up, I gave em a
swift whack! I made sure
they were clean-cut,
did their chores and
went to church. I don't
know what went wrong,

but this new generation,
God knows, they're different.
My older boy ran away, and
the last I heard, he's married
a woman twice his age!
The younger one, Ricky, he is
doing better, but not a whole lot.
He dropped out of school and
roams around smoking pot."

218
"I'm sorry to hear that,
Mr. Ladderman. Raising children
is a tricky business, it seems.
Damned if you do and
damned if you don't, as
you folks might say;
you have to hit the right
balance. As you put it,
mindless mollycoddling
misses the point,
just as the barn shed and
the birch rod routine
could also backfire."

219
"Loving guidance, on the
other hand, should give
lasting results. By that I
mean, do things such that
you flood your child's heart
with love and his mind
with rules! All of which calls
for time and devotion by
the parents, and teamwork

between husband and wife.
Oh, I didn't mean to lecture
you, Mr. Ladderman.
Besides, I don't yet have
my own children to speak of"
said Vijay, pulling back.
Officer Lawrence Ladderman
sat down, seeming near
the breaking point.

220
"No, your words make good sense, doctor.
I didn't tell you what's really been
killing me. My wife is wanting
to take the girls and leave me.
I just can't bear the thought of
them leaving me . . ."
Vijay handed some tissue to
the uniformed prison guard,
walked over and shut the door,
to allow the older man sob
silently. Dabbing the tears flowing
freely from his facial cavities,
Mr. Ladderman suddenly
seemed frail and infirm.

221
"I hate to take up your time—
I know you have inmates to see.
But ever since the boys
went bad, I stopped going
to church and been drinking
too much. My wife,
Molly is her name—bless her heart—
she says she's scared

to be around me
and blames me for what happened . . ."

222
Mr. Ladderman concludes:
"I have been a God-fearing
and hard-working man
all my life, just as my
Daddy taught me. All I ever
did was work in this prison,
besides some farming on
the side—I have a few
acres of tobacco. When I
was younger, I was
a volunteer with the county
fire department and active
in the church. When the kids
were little, we were a real
happy family. But those days
seem so far away . . ."

223
"Now, I'm afraid my world is
upside down.
I can still handle it, as long
as Molly doesn't leave me.
I know she still loves me, and
so do the girls. But their mind
is with Robert and Ricky,
about whom they blame me.
I'm worried too, doctor—
I hate for the boys to end up
in this here prison, of all places . . ."

Inner City Patricide

This poem describes an inner city tragedy in which Rashad, one of Sheila's tenth grade pupils, murders his father, who has abused Rashad's mother all her life. Young Rashad is arrested and taken to the prison where Vijay works as a psychologist.

224
"Hello, Vijju. Sorry to disturb you at work.
I just had to call someone,
something terrible happened!"
"Sheila, honey, are you OK?
Tell me, what happened?" asked
Vijay, anxiously. "Rashad—he is
a boy from my class—they say
he shot and killed his father,
early this morning. It was on
the 12 o'clock news!"
Vijay: "Oh, my God, that's
just terrible. I hate to say this,
but it sounds like
one of my cases, here in this prison!"
Sheila: "That's what I told Tasha.
Mr. Moody, our principal, said
they might send young Rashad
to your Castlegate prison
for detention.
Do they have place
for such young fellows?"
"Well, we do have a safekeeper block,
where they house juveniles
awaiting trial, once in a while.

They put them
in a single cell by themselves,
so no one puts their hands
on them. I'm sorry, darling,
you folks are having a
rough day. I'll see you at home.
Bye now!" Vijay hung up.

Rashad's Reverberations

Rashad's teachers, Sheila and Tasha, are deeply disturbed by the murder committed by their young pupil. Sheila is highly affected and entertains doubts about her academic mission, and gives in to other misgivings. She contacts her mother in India and seeks comfort. Sheila and Vijay have to get away— so they go on a short vacation to nearby Asheville, NC.

225
Tasha was in tears,
and Sheila ws dejected.
They cancelled the
afternoon class, and declared
self-study in the library.
"Tasha, it's not your fault what
happened. Neither you nor Clarisse,
the Social Worker, could've
done anything more than what
you already have."
Tasha didn't reply. She hung her
head down and kept pressing
the cloth kerchief against the tears.
Sheila continued: "I was noticing
that Rashad had been absent
more than usual, in the last month.
What's strange, his class work had
actually improved and he'd been talking
to me more freely. I couldn't tell
anything was wrong."

226
Tasha looked up, her face
flushed from the crying.
"That's the problem with
all these children;
they don't communicate!
I suppose so much is troubling
them; plus, they don't have
intimacy with anyone—not
enough to develop trust.
Every time I talk to these kids,
I have to *pry* the information
and feelings out of them.
Why, the whole thing is
a crying shame!"
Tasha gave in to
another wave of grief.

227
It didn't take
but a moment;
and one shot
into the heart
of his father
who fell back
and died.
Boom.
Silence.

228
Rashad just stood there,
glued by gravity,
looking down; at death.
For the first time

in his life,
he did something;
accomplished something;
something real;
that just lay there,
dead.
The gun;
it just killed...his father.
Rashad dropped it,
and walked out.

229
Many sounds and footsteps.
People, cars, commotion.
They put on handcuffs,
and metal chains;
and jerked him around.
He didn't feel a thing.
He never did, and not now.
He was sliding into a dream.
He felt like a ravished rag doll.
His mind was receding
into himself,
like tide water between toes.
'Am I dying?'
He didn't much care.

230
Stuff happens before you know it.
All it takes
is an emotional earthling
on one end,
and one whose time has come,
on the other; in the middle:

a 38-caliber, hollow point,
hollow-minded Court TV society!"

231
Sheila was very distraught
and deeply disturbed.
She was pacing,
beyond her helper-husband's ken.
Diagnosis: Adjustment Disorder to-the-inner
city-realities-of-the-only-superpower.
Mode of Treatment: Any of the thousand and
one brands of Gomax.
Side Effects: possible, but not probable,
aggravation
of each and every presenting symptom, and,
at least, one in a
billion patients may commit suicide—sorry.
Oh, yeah, the FDA is aware.
Rehabilitation: Go back to Bangalore, India.
Prognosis: Dicey.

232
Sheila's typically calm and
calculating mind was rioting.
Why has she made
this bargain with the devil?
Why did she choose
to move all the way to America?
And throw herself into
the thick of their problems!
As if she was a Bollywood heroine
going to the rescue of the downtrodden;
like Shabana Azmi in a
socially uplifting role?!

There she was, a happy,
hymn-singing
Secondary School teacher,
in her friendly, familiar Bangalore;
with stable, overprotected,
and highly respected antecedents.

233
What was she thinking?
For that matter, first of all,
why did she even agree to marry?!
She looked at Vijay, plumped
down in the ugly yellow sofa,
unshaven, glancing distractedly
at a glossy ad for ADD medicine.
She felt a pang of guilt.

234
Sheila was on satellite-aided
telephone with her mother, all night,
which was all day for Shobha
Murthy, stuck in Malleswaram
Time Zone. "Shiloo, puttu, why
don't you both come away, back to
Bangalore? You can get fine jobs,
right here. Haven't you heard
all the American jobs are
coming here to Bangalore?!
Anyway, why is that? Are
those Americans also getting
lazy like those Sheiks in
Saudi, who sit around and
smoke their hazy water pipes?"

235
Shobha digressed;
Sheila became irritated
at her mother, an old habit
she missed. "Mummy, stop
talking about America
and India and jobs, as if
you are a big politician!
I am tired of both countries.
Just be my music-loving mom,
who cooks fine, vegetarian,
Kannada *oota* and is
always there for me!"

236
"OK, *Baaba*, okay... I'm sorry.
Of course, I am always
here for you, Shiloo. So
is your father, you know that.
He's right here, would you
like to talk to him?"
said Shobha Murthy.
Her husband,
Prof. Manjunath Murthy,
was anxiously pacing.
"No, tell him I'm fine. I know
he gets so worried. Don't tell
him about what all is going
on in our jobs, here in America;
he would want us to pack
up and leave, right now!"

237
"Of course, part of me is
always thinking of going back,

but the other half wants to
stay and deal with the
challenges—they call it
the American Spirit, God knows!
Anyway, mummy, I'm already
feeling better, thank you. Sorry,
I worried you. I love you,
I'll be fine. Bye."

238
Vijay and Sheila, Sanskrit for
Victor and Chastity respectively,
go on their first American vacation;
to nearby Asheville, NC, home of
The Biltmore House,
a colonial palace
where a crownless king once
smoked lazy cigars.
They ate Chinese ("Vegetable Fried
Rice, no egg, please!" "Just water,
no ice, please!" they ordered, in unison)
and later took in a G-rated
Disney dispensation. They
quibbled about tobacco
traces in their certified,
non-smoking motel room,
but otherwise enjoyed
the southern hospitality.
Sheila rested and felt more relaxed,
as they returned to Bull City,
playing a *Bala Murali* CD.

Rewriting the Rulebook

A deeply frustrated and disillusioned prison
inmate who feels victimized by the raw deal
he has received in life, denounces life itself.

239
"If I could rewrite the rulebook,
your ass will be the first to go!"
(Unidentified inmate, ranting at
the nearest officer.)
"But there are more urgent issues;
let's get to the bottom of
this entire mess they call life!
I hate to say this, but
there should be a law
against people shackin' up
and havin' babies,
like a pair of stray dogs
in heat. My folks were in
no position to take care of me—
hell, they couldn't take care
of their own damn selves!
I was knocked from pillar to
post, and I wasn't even nine.
Grandparents, foster parents,
therapeutic halfway homes,
I made the rounds of all
the half-assed houses
in the state.
I was as tired of putting up
with them, as they were
of dealing with me."

240

"I finally found the people
who *could* deal with anyone.
I mean, drug dealers in
street corners who
welcomed me with open
arms and enclosed fists.
Well, the rest is history.
Yep, they oughta rewrite
the rulebook and stop
punishing victims
a second round. Why,
the whole thing is *bizarre*!"

What Will Happen to Rashad?

Following the arrest of Rashad for the murder of his father, MLK High goes into turmoil. The principal calls a special assembly, and later Sheila' class holds a discussion group. Sheila's psychologist-husband Vijay, who works at the prison, attempts to look up Rashad to monitor his status and reports back to Sheila.

241
Mr. Moody called a special assembly.
All of MLK High gathered in the gym,
where bold lettering on the wall
still proclaimed, *"A Mind is a
Terrible Thing to Waste."*
Mr. Moody stepped onto the podium
under the basketball hoop,
and made fresh proclamations,
stating what happened was sad,
"any which way you look at it,"
he asserted. "For a son, to kill
his father! You wonder
what brought it on."
Rashad Richardson was
a good kid, a member of the
school basketball team
"who used to play right here,
where you all are standing!"
"But I don't care what nobody
says... hand the kid a gun,
and you're asking for trouble.
We've got too many guns,
too much violence,

and we've *got* to put
a stop to this!"

242
Mr. Moody, tribal chief of this
African American academic
assemblage, finished addressing
his flock. What he *didn't* say
was, "I don't know why our
lives are the way they are.
Why do we have so many
murders 'Black on Black?'
Why are we still disenfranchised,
a century after slavery?
I'm just a figurehead figure,
walking around wearing a suit;
a minority, who made it into
the Middle Class, where it feels
lavish yet lonely when I look
back on the Pettigrew Street projects..."

243
Sheila tried to cajole the class
to concentrate on precalculus.
But the kids, aggravated by
Mr. Moody's assembly,
were still reeling from
the Rashad reverberations.
Sheila stopped, looked at Tasha,
who looked down.
Elaine, the eager college volunteer,
took the initiative and
asked the class, "Would you
all want to discuss

what happened with Rashad?"
Many in the class nodded their
assent, whereupon Elaine looked
at Sheila, who, in turn, nodded
her consent. "Who wants to
go first?" asked Elaine,
relishing her new leadership role.

244
Mikela's hand shot up.
"Does anyone know why
he shot his dad?" The others
chimed in, "Yeah, how come no one
tells us what really went down?"
"Are they going to kill him, on Death Row?
One of my uncles is in prison,
on Death Row..." remarked Rufus,
who rarely spoke.
"I heard on TV that Rashad was upset
because his dad was into beatin'
on his mother,"
said Jasper, jerking his knees.
A girl surmised, "Maybe Rashad
was in a gang. How come
he had a gun?" At which,
an up-and-coming
'Nattering Nabob of Negativism'
jeered at her, saying, "you don't
need to be in no gang to
get hold of no gun!
Besides, I know Rashad—he
wasn't gang bangin'." That was
Jayron, the three-hundred
pound man-child and football tackle.

The kids processed,
while the teachers stood by,
looking more pensive than apprehensive.

245
Vijay's computer at work
corroborated Sheila's—Rashad
held captive at
Castlegate Correctional:
RICHARDSON, RASHAD RAHMAN
#R04238: AWAITING TRIAL
MURDER IN THE FIRST DEGREE
blinked the blue screen.
D.O.B. 3-3-1986
RACE: AFRICAN AMERICAN
OCCUPATION: TENTH GRADE
The Corrections computer was
oblivious to the Vijay-Sheila
connection, and otherwise
clueless about the surrounding
human melodrama.
No room for such soft stuff
on a prison hard drive,
Vijay had to concede.
An early transfer—from the
yellow school bus to the
white prison bus—
to languish behind prison walls,
and relive his childhood over
and over, till it's all over.
Goodbye, Martin Luther King High.

246
Vijay pressed the button at the

entrance to the seg. building,
and waited patiently.
Patience rewarded, he walked into
the private quarters of men
who were assigned to
"the prison within prison."
He ambled toward D-Pod,
where they housed undertrial
safekeepers, who were
made to look distinct,
shod in a disturbing shade of red.
The sliding steel door opened
for the mental health doctor
on a semi-private house call.
Vijay went in and stood in front of
the corner cell. Richardson was
lying down on his bunk.
He lifted his head, peered
at the visitor, turned, and
went back to sleep—
to the preferred prison pastime.

247
"Actually, there isn't much to report.
Rashad's there, alright—I went
and saw him today. He wouldn't
talk to me, or anyone else for
that matter, according to the
officers on the block.
He's eating his meals, though,
and comes out to shower,
but that's about it," Vijay informed
Sheila, who was sitting at
the kitchen table grading exams.

"His family, I mean his
mother and sister, visited
him on Sunday. According to
the officers, Rashad didn't
say much; they all sat there,
crying. Maybe, he will
open up to you folks from
the school, who can tell?
I'll ask Warden
Hardison for permission."
Sheila looked up, and
nodded her thanks.

Sheila's Class Goes on a Scared Straight Program

The tenth graders, accompanied by their
teachers, go on a field trip to Castlegate
Correctional Center where their fallen
comrade Rashad is detained. This segment
describes the reactions of the pupils and their
teachers to the harsh realities of
incarceration. The poem ends poignantly
when the group has to say a quick hello and
hasty goodbye to young Rashad, who is not
free to return with them.

248
Sheila's 10th graders
went on a Scared Straight Program.
Victoria Verwoerd, the vice principal,
Tasha, the teacher's assistant, and
Sheila, the ever sensible,
South Indian math import,
together led the sixteen,
peer-pressured, baggy-bottomed
guys, and balloon-bosomed gals,
into the foyer of the fortress
which is the CCC.
The field trip triggered
tangled emotions in the
African American adolescents—
fear, chief among them.
And many questions:
What's prison like? Are the people sad?
Do they get beatings? They get good food?
How old is the youngest guy in here?

Where do they keep Rashad?
Will we get to see him?

249
Sergeant Blount received the group
and quickly took charge.
"Who is this chunky monkey?" Brevard
whispered to Kenyon, before he was shushed
by Ms. Verwoerd, who felt
clearly outranked by the
disciplining demeanor of the
burly Blount. When he started
barking, the suddenness of it
took the whole group by surprise.
Sheila was simply shocked,
having never witnessed
such a tirade. Tasha was puzzled,
and gazed at the young charges,
gauging their reaction.
Ms. Verwoerd was deeply impressed
by the embodied authority, to
which she secretly aspired.
The kids just stood there,
rooted, with their hands deep
inside their baggy pockets.

250
"Call it a penitentiary or penal institution,
a correctional facility, or by
any other fancy designation—
you can't escape from the
fact that this is an ugly old prison!
It's a sad place,
full of bad men: murderers,

molesters, and misguided ministers—
we've got them all in here,
living sadly ever after.
We crack down hard on those
who buck the system, play games,
or run rackets.
We bust up gangs, and
prevent prostitution.
We'll do whatever it takes
to maintain peace and order
in here!" (Order, maybe;
peace? No way, thought
Tasha, feeling the negative vibe
coming from her flock.)

251
"I see you young buckaroos,
breaking the law and
bustin' down prison doors!
Think twice before you
join the Wrong Crowd.
I don't wanna hear about
you bein' in the wrong place,
at the wrong time—this here
is the wrongest place there
could be! And it never
is the right time to come in here!
Do you wanna be robbed, attacked,
and otherwise degraded
and humilified?
Far worse things happen,
but I won't get into those, being
we're in mixed company.
And you, in the yellow T-shirt!

I know the look. You think you're
a tough guy, a gangsta thug?
Would you like to meet up
with some rough dudes?
I can arrange that—they
can't wait to meet little
teat-suckers like you!"

252
Blount's broadside had the
predictable effect.
The kids shut down, and
the teachers were tongue-tied.
Sheila started sweating, and
Tasha was trembling.
Verwoerd, the Vice Principal,
was wordless in awe.
It was a rare moment of
all-round awkwardness,
a perfect paralysis
in the prison-public protocol.
A gagging gridlock, where
no one could make a move,
not even Blount, never mind
Brevard. You can say too much,
and scare them only so much.
The awkward silence was, at last,
broken by a foreign accent—
a cheerful British greeting,
by way of Bangalore.

253
"Hi, there, Sergeant Blount,
hello, people! I'm Dr. Bhaskar—

that's right, your teacher Sheila's
proud husband. I happen to
work here, I'm a psychologist.
You kids know what that is?"
Vijay asked, trying to relate.
(Sheila was glad to see Vijay,
detecting a more assertive
self in him, reserved only
for prison?)
"You help people,
those who have problems,
don't you?" offered Latoya,
the daughter of a recovered
drug addict.
"That's right, and
it keeps me busy.
Sergeant Blount will
probably agree," said Vijay,
glancing toward the Bull Dog Blount,
who flashed a
conspiratorial grin.
"Blount is a busy man,
besides, he's training for the
Mr. Correctional Weightlifting Championship,
so we don't want to be
in his way. Thank you, Sergeant,
I'll take over from here."
Blount moved on,
but not before treating Brevard
to a much-practiced parting stare.
Brevard, deeply
disturbed within, kept up his
air of bravado, mumbling,
"Man, that dude's crazy!"

What mattered was, Blount
was relieved, and so were
the visitors.
"Well, Sergeant Blount
isn't our worst, but he surely
has a style of his own.
Let's talk about the inmates,
not staff. I know you're all
eager to see your friend Rashad.
But there are a thousand
others in here
besides your buddy.
What brings all these people
to prison?" prodded Vijay.

254
He engaged the youngsters
in basic prison sociology:
poverty, deprivation,
disenfranchisement,
alienation, and all other
ailments of uncouth, urban living.
The abstract, academic treatment
of life in horrorhood
sailed right over the heads of the
assembled youth, who had little
idea that Vijay was talking about *them*—
their lives and daily experiences.
They' eager to go in,
look around the prison, and
meet its cheerless inhabitants.
Joined by Samantha Sealy,
Programs Specialist, Vijay led
the group towards the dormitories.

255
They walk in a single file,
the girls following the boys.
They walk into a dorm
full of drab-looking men,
who lift their heads and
look on wearily.
Some come up to the glass,
peer at the young guys and girls,
and manage a manly smile,
however wanly.
Neither side is certain
who's on display.
That the Child is Father
of the Man—neither the children
nor the men are aware.
They happen to meet
in this strange barracks
built for bad soldiers,
AWOL from life.
They recognize each other,
see each other in each other,
as wilderness meets captivity.

256
They are shown the chow hall,
and the chapel; walk by the
warden's offices; peek into
the prison's own high school,
where bearded men are
learning basic math.
The time comes for the visitors
to walk to Segregation,
where, they're told, Rashad

Richardson is housed.
They wait for the sliding
metal doors to open,
gingerly walk down
the hallway and gather
on the ground floor,
looking up at the three tiers
of prison cells.
They're pointed toward
the second-tier corner,
where Rashad is standing
behind his steel door.
He can see them,
but they can't see him.
Soon, he can't see his
friends either, for the
flooding tears.
Vijay escorts Sheila and
Tasha up the stairs,
while Verwoerd stayed back
with the flock.
They pass other men,
seated in their cells,
before stopping
at Rashad's.

257
There he stands, right behind
the door, looking through
the long, narrow aperture.
He's crying, shaking his head,
his body racking with grief.
You see, his life just died,
and he's finding it hard

to go on without it.
Tasha just breaks down,
shaking with sobs,
while Sheila grabs hold of her.
Vijay leads them back
down the winding metal stairs.
The huddled group from
MLK High looks up
one last time toward
their fallen comrade,
and waves him goodbye, for real.

Derrick Drucker Crosses a Line

A moving and powerful tale from the bowels of a high-security prison. An inmate is driven to mucking with his body waste, just to obtain the administrators' fleeting attention. The poem ends on a positive note, after the inmate is made to feel personally acknowledged by the psychologist who is called to the scene.

258
"Dr. Bhaskar? This is Gross—
Grosvenor Gunn. Can you
walk down to Foxtrot,
lower level? Our man
Drucker, who else, is
makin' a scene. It's a classic
prison standoff,
a great on-the-job-op
for you?!" said the
Associate Warden for the
High Control Unit, an
amiable, beer-slurping,
club-wielder, and an
ally of Vijay's in
the Administration.
Vijay stopped the dictation,
sucked on the water bottle
and set off toward the
serious part of prison—
called the SuperSeg.

259
It was a pretty fall morning.
The rec yard was busy;
the banging backboards,
clink of horseshoes,
and the crashing barbells
at the weight pile
lent an air of freedom, vigor,
and human enterprise, under
pastel powder-blue skies.
"Even the convicts are happy
on a day like this!" Vijay heard
a peppy prison guard quip.

260
Gunn and the guards were
gathered in front of Drucker's
high-security cell.
It was a morbid sight.
Darkish fecal matter
smeared all over the walls,
especially on the glass
surface. It was hard to
make out that Drucker
was standing at the
door—naked.
Vijay wished he had carried
a cotton kerchief
to cover his nose
from the sordid smell.
On the glass pane were
letters held to be holy,
etched in excrement.
A compelling sight—it worked;

it brought the bigwigs
into the block, cutting
through layers of the
administration's apathy.

261
Drucker crossed a line, that day;
silently shattered the
sound barrier, so to speak.
He ignored instinct and
innate inhibition.
Now forty-two, he knew better
than to muck around
since he was two.
It's one's own—an intimate,
yet alien part-and-parcel
of everyday life;
it's proof one is alive,
however repugnant;
it's successful refuse,
a byproduct of
a brilliant biological process—
a necessary evil.
Truth be told, Drucker
didn't feel his life
was better than the pile of shit.
Probably worse, he would say.
He's himself an unsuccessful
heap of refuse;
an insane side effect of a
shameful societal process—
an unnecessary evil,
worse than night soil.
He is repugnant even to

himself. A severely
compromised self-esteem
leads to blurring of lines
and a fracture of
the boundary walls.
What of self and what of others,
and where's the question of esteem?!

262
Yet still, the business of State
has to go on.
"I don't care, what kind of
complaint he's got... He can't
be smearing shit and stuff!
He can't be *dictating* any
which way he wants to"
fumed Gunn, the legitimate
designated dictator, on hand.
Vijay, who's still cutting his
teeth in the business of running
American prisons, suggested
he would attempt a dialogue with
the bacterially-barricaded-bank robber.
"But first, we should allow
him to shower, be given
a fresh pair of clothes,
and moved to the
Meeting Room,"
demanded the demi-daring doctor
from the Heat-and-Dust East.
The associate Warden
allowed Vijay's wishes,
and barked out orders
to the blue-shirted guards.

263
Derrick Drucker was escorted
by a posse of prison guards.
He looked clean—freshly
showered and shaved;
he walked like a prize
fighter with his entourage.
He stood behind the
plexiglass partition,
with his hands cuffed
behind him.
Vijay spoke into the metal
amplifier, to get through.
"Mr. Drucker, hi. You remember
me, don't you? I'm Dr. Vijay Bhaskar,
Psychologist. What happened?
Why did you do it?
Do you want to tell me?"
Looking somewhat sheepish,
Drucker replied:
"I hated to do it, but
I had no choice.
You know how it is
around here.
No one seems to care!"

264
 "Look, I don't know how much
you know about what goes on here.
I *do* know you're a New Jack!
They probably brainwashed you
with all kinds of lies.
But you look like
you're a good man,

so I'll level with you.
As you can see, they treat us like shit.
The few things we're
entitled to, by law, they
deny us. Take legal mail,
for instance. They aren't
supposed to mess with it.
Yet, I swear to you, I
don't get half the stuff my
lawyer sends me. I've
got a lawsuit going for
feeding me Putriment.
They punish you with that
piece of cardboard—have
you ever tasted it? Golly...
I'm gonna win this thing,
'cause I have a peptic ulcer
which *they've* been
treating for years—they
can't feed me no Putriment!
I write complaints and
grievances—but no one responds.
Well, this place is enough
to drive a man crazy!"

265
Vijay knows the score.
He does know what
time it is.
Gunn is short-staffed,
and running the place
half-cocked.
No time,
no funds for training.

206

New hires don't stay
long enough to receive
their first paycheck.
The bad ones stay on and
add to the problems.
It's a no-win situation—
a pet phrase of Gross Gunn.

266
"I hear you, Mr. Drucker. It
sounds like we haven't
been doing you right.
I'll talk to Mr.Gunn
regarding your mail.
As far as your special meal—
'Medicinal Meal' is
what they call it—
it's up to the Dietary
Review Committee.
I'll inform them
of your marginal medical status,
and see if they couldn't
put you back on regular
food.
They told me it had
to do with your throwing
urine on an officer?
But you say that's in the past..."

267
"Why don't you have
a hot meal? I'm
recommending that
they not give you

what you refer to
as Putriment or whatever, today.
Go back and GI your
cell, real clean. They'll
help hose it down
for you.
And remember:
don't mess with
body waste in future—
You could come down
with Hepatitis!"

268
All Drucker needed was
Acknowledgement,
if not Acceptance;
even a gesture would do,
by someone who was
attentive and sympathetic.
He began whistling and
singing Home on the Range,
as he scrubs away the scum,
wearing yellow rubber gloves.
Yes, all one needs is some
soap and water, and
a little TLC!
It's so elementary,
perhaps too much so—
because no training, no
workshop, nor college course
mentions acceptance as
the overarching principle.
Make it golden, platinum,
or any precious metal.

All Creation is yearning to
be accepted.
Accepted as presented, period.
Accepted on one's terms,
in one's own light and right.
It's like "it's not about you,
this is about *me*! See what
I have come to be—take a look,
take a good look–see!"

A Blast From the Information Explosion!

This lighthearted segment pokes fun at sensationalism in the American media. The not so good news one finds in the newspapers knocks out Vijay, on a casual trip to the local library.

269
Vijay went with Sheila
to the county library.
While she was checking
out leads to matters
mathematical,
he spent time perusing papers
and periodicals. *The New York Times,
Chicago Tribune, Washington Post*,
and from the West Coast, *The LA Times*.
Time zones vary, but not
the tidings. The fonts and
fancy trappings aside,
the facts are very same:
that the world's going to hell
in a handbasket.
"Tough economic times ahead!"
warns the wailing
Wall Street Journal.
"The terrorists are coming!"
threatens *The Teaneck Tea
Time Tribune*.
"The oceans are getting old,
criminals getting young!"
cries out *The Albany Alarmist*.

270
Vijay got up to use the
facilities, and walked over
to the vending machines,
where cultivated
capitalism dispensed
a chocolate-peanut confection,
in fancy biodegradable foil.
Back in the news
section, the periodicals
were less in-your-face.
The erudite *Economist*
examined the Middle Eastern
mind, while *The Reader's Digest*
regurgitated washed up,
old world bromides.
For its part,
The National Geographic
explored the extinction facing
Egyptian muskrat.

271
Vijay, along with Sheila,
wobbled out, barely surviving
the blast from the Information
Explosion.
"Let's go home
and drink hot Darjeeling tea.
I have some *chhat* to go with it."
suggested Sheila.
"*There's* some good news, at last!"
chuckled V. Vijay Bhaskar.

Sheila Bhaskar, The Math Buster!

This short segment describes the innovative efforts of Sheila to expose students in her math class to a variety of intellectual experiences and thereby gear them towards academic success.

272
The End of Grades are
approaching, the semester
a few weeks from well-done.
Sheila was honored as
Ms. Innovation, by the
planners and specialists
in the Central Office.
MLK High, by itself,
doesn't recognize
meritorious cases,
decreeing that all teachers
are created equal in the
eyes of the principal.
Sheila's Sixteen have been
very busy, what with chess
games and music practice
as after school assignments.

273
The children were awakened
to the finer sides of their minds,
thrilling secretly in
intellectual exertion.
Edwardo excelled at chess,

giving his college coaches
a run for their money.
The early-evening extracurricular
explorations were yielding
academic dividends, in the
mid-morning math marathons.
274
Brother Yusef, the music teacher,
worked closely with Sheila Bhaskar,
the Math Buster; he enrolled
extra assistants from the
university music department.
Alongside Scott Joplin and
Duke Ellington, they now
practiced piano concertos
of Bach and Beethoven!
Other instruments flourished too—
the sax, trumpet, and the violin,
to wit.
Steady and continuous
practice of musical
manipulations, resulted in
gratifying gains; attuning,
in the process, the moribund
minds to purpose, discipline,
and formality.
The shallow
and superficial slowly
gave way to succinct and
sound reasoning, adding gravitas
to the young, growing minds.

275
In another cool deal,
a small cadre of girls

signed up to learn *Carnatic*
vocal, under Sheila's tutelage.
Vijay laughed at the very
idea, adding to Sheila's
secret doubts.
But she took
up the challenge to teach the
bashful black girls, twice
a week, *Swarams, raagams*
and *geethams*.
There was
much frustration and laughter,
before it too seemed like
any math exercise: calling
for concentration, clarity,
and engagement of the
faculties.
One girl
gravitated to the *Veena*,
claiming better aptitude
for man-made instruments,
than God-given *gaathram*.

Arrivals and Departures

Vijay walks over and watches inmate activity in the Reception/Transportation area of the prison. He observes some inmates who are in the process of leaving prison, having completed their long, hard years of incarceration; and others, who are just arriving, to begin their own lengthy ordeals lying ahead of them.

276
Vijay walked over to Transportation,
to observe the comings and
goings into and out of prison;
into and out of the
minor modular hell.
The arrivals and departures
occur on the hour,
of the calcified *Karmic* Clock.
Vijay couldn't help but notice
the cruel touch of the
clear plexiglass partition
between the comers and goers;
"Fresh Meat" glancing longingly
through the glass at shapeless,
but not hapless humanoids,
taxiing at the Departure Gate.
Alas, it takes twenty-odd years
to claw through the glass,
crossover, and fly into a fitful future.

PTA at MLK

PTA night at Sheila's school. Only a few parents are present to learn about their children's academic progress. However, Sheila's class is the exception—Tasha, her conscientious assistant, spares no effort to drum up parental attendance. The principal congratulates Sheila on her good work, and, back at home, Vijay echoes the heaps of praise.

277
It was Wednesday night.
PTA at MLK, but not many takers.
The teachers are ready,
just in case, to defend and distance
themselves from falling scores
and failing grades, neatly
charted into sliced pies
and sliding curves.
"It's a bit late in the day
for Johnny to jump-start
his Language Arts—he's
in the 11th grade!
We recommend he go into
arc welding or some such
thing," suggested
Mr. Frank Forthright, a
frustrated Fulbright Scholar.
Single mothers working
double jobs, doing
domestic duty;

checking on their kids,
circumspect of their prospects.

278
Sheila's Algebra class, as always,
was anomalous.
Tasha, who's been in constant touch
with the mothers,
made sure they showed up
in good numbers.
"Look, Ms. McCombs,
you have to attend!
Mario is doing so well,
you'll be proud!"
she urged them.
Mr. Moody, the principal,
was heartened to see
the bustle and bright lights
of 10th Grade Math.
A piano was rolled in,
for a special revue;
in a corner, Edwardo and
the egghead collegians
were pondering, pawns in hand.
Sheila's homemade *pakoras*
went very well with
the organic apple juice.

279
"How do you do it, Ms. Bhaskar?
I've been a teacher all my life,
but I never saw anyone take
such interest in teaching kids;
especially at the high school

level. I mean, beyond the
call of duty!" gushed
Mr. Moody, looking
admiringly at
Ms. Innovation.
Sheila blushed, feeling very good,
if a trifle embarrassed.
"Thank you, Mr. Moody,
you're just being nice.
Tasha is the one who
keeps me going.
And the kids, they respond to warmth
and affection, like flowers
to sunlight.
Besides, I can't do it without
your support,"
said Sheila, making
another Awards Night
Acceptance Speech.

280
"I just can't believe
what all is happening.
That I am married and
working in America,
teaching disadvantaged
children.
That everyone
is so nice to me,
Black, White, I mean,
everyone.
Sometimes, I
feel a bit guilty; after all,

I just got here,
a flat-out foreigner!
I feel so grateful for
all the support I receive
from the American people,
never mind, I am still
an unknown quantity."

281
Vijay put down the newspaper
and looked up at Sheila,
and remarked:
"I've been thinking too,
about your
phenomenal success
with the kids, in your
very first year.
My dear bride,
if I might also confide,
that makes me feel much pride.
But back to the issue
at hand. It's really you,
pure and simple.
Your patient,
supportive approach; your
persistent and preplanned
pedagogy, all have
obviously paid off!"
prattled the prison practitioner.
Sheila, obviously pleased,
laughed teasingly at Vijay,
saying, "*Enu* Vijju, what's up?
You're in a blatantly
buttering mood today!"

Holes in Their Escape Plans

A short, semi-humorous poem, on the shattered hopes of inmates eyeing the prison fence...

282
Vijay arrived at the
prison parking lot,
got out of the
compliant Corolla,
adjusted his tie,
and about to reach in
for his briefcase and
bottle of water,
when he heard a
fusillade of gunfire—
nonstop rapid fire,
not from afar.
Unexpected sound
effects, early in the day.
The chickadees stopped
chirping, and the crows
suffered a cardiac.
The prison mates knew
by an instinct even the
real birds lacked:
the guards were at the
Firing Range, shooting
automatic weapons;
firing holes into
foolproof escape plans,
leaving human hope
in smoldering ruins!

Country Prison in Crestridge County

This is a tragic tale of a botched escape attempt from a high-security prison, undertaken by a few inexperienced and youthful inmates. Even though it was a temporary duty assignment for Vijay, the traumatic incident made it memorable.

283
Vijay was assigned away from
Castlegate Correctional Center
for a month, subbing for
a fellow Freudian
who was savoring a
sojourn in the South of France.
The new prison, Crestridge,
was a maximum-security
affair for youth and
young adults—rowdies and
rascals, at the peak of
their powers.
The daily drive into
the countryside, on sunny
summer mornings, was
welcome variety; through
cedar groves and forest oaks,
past cow pastures and
placid ponds, listening
to Rachmaninoff
on Public Radio.
Destination: Country Prison
in Crestridge County.

284
The caseload was heavy
with the burdens of
broken youth.
Young colts
and wild mustangs,
barricaded inside
solitary stables.
Personality Disorders,
pronounce the shrinks;
pain-in-the-butts,
dismiss the prison guards.
"You can't take your eyes off
of 'em, nary for a minute!"
cautioned the crusty caretakers.
Vijay found the kids to be lively,
even friendly, for the most part,
during the one-on-one chit-chats.
In front of their precarious peers,
however, it's another matter.
They had to maintain mean,
malevolent facades,
and defend their putative,
predatory profiles.

285
They're the marginalized
members of
a misguided gang of
young brigands,
made to sit around
and idle away
the mornings,
musing on missed opportunities

with merry-go-lucky lasses.
Their lives suspended,
their letters rebounded,
bored to death,
and tired of running
their mouths; they're
a rowdy group
of wretched American boys,
on a long timeout,
without any play toys.
"I want some volunteers
to mow the lawn,
fertilize, and sow
grass seed!" hollered
the skinny old sergeant,
squinting through
the trapdoor.
They sprang to their feet,
put on their cleats,
and romped to the waiting
prison-brand push mowers.
They fired up the engines
and manhandled
the hungry lawn eaters,
recalling the sweet smells
of childhood grasses...

286
It was an agreeable
midsummer day.
A crisp morning, with
birds in the air, and dew
on the ground.
The young men in prison

couldn't escape feeling
frenetic in their bones.
They poured out into the
play area, throwing, pressing,
prancing, and pushing against
the grass; running away
from concrete confinement.
The shots rang out
suddenly,
arresting all activity;
especially the two
who were
climbing brazenly
up the barbed wire fence.

287
Leave it two ill-advised
youth, to try and break
out of prison at ten
on a 20/20 morning;
from right under the
snarling barrel
of a 12-gauge shotgun!

Both were hit,
and felled to the ground.
One dead.

He lay inert
in a prison T-shirt,
with a pink tincture
seeping from a puncture
freshly made.

Vijay, who was close by,
rushed out to the
surreal scene, and ordered water
for the gasping survivor.
Two other young fools,
part of the botched breakout,
were hugging the damp earth
for dear life.

288
"They weren't seeking freedom;
it was glory, they were after;
glory, in front of their co-captives,"
Vijay advised the officials,
later that day.
"Martyrdom is a sweet madness,
it's seductive self-sacrifice;
heedlessness dubbed heroism,
a pathetic path to Paradise.
The youth are easy prey
to instant, irreversible
self-dissolution..."
Bill Adderly, the kid
who perished,
fit the bill of a restless
renegade, Vijay recalled.
Paradise or not, he
certainly eluded prison
and its timeless techniques
of tyranny.

289
In a further fit of irony,
it was later revealed that

the EMT who rushed
to the scene, and bandaged
the bleeding survivor,
was none other than the
kid brother of Officer
Harry Hooter, our
deadeye sharpshooter!
One brother butchered,
and the other sutured?
Nah, if anything, Mr. Hooter,
whom Vijay later debriefed,
was riddled with grief.
The horrified Hooter,
a mild-mannered son
of a Bible Belt farmer,
was sad and disconsolate.

290
Months later, back in business
at Castlegate CC,
Vijay's phone rang.
It was a young woman,
nervous, with a country accent—
deftly diagnosed Dr. Bhaskar.
"Were you the doctor,
who was counselin' Bill Adderely
before he was shot?"
the lady timidly inquired.
Vijay answered in the
affirmative.
"I was his wife—I'm sorry,
his ex-wife; we got
divorced. I'm Kimberly.
I'm just curious. Did Billy

mention my name?
Did he ever say
he loved me?" she queried.
"He most certainly did!"
lied the con-doctor.

291
Many lives are running
all at once,
like movies at a Multiplex.
From titles to credits,
they run their course.
After a week or two,
at the most,
the reel is rewound
and replaced in its box,
and carted away
to the cobwebs.
When lives intersect
as they invariably do,
there's pleasure, even
passion which pass on,
leaving the sediment of
wounded sentiment.

The Night of Shiva

Sheila and Vijay celebrate the all-night Hindu festival of worshipping Lord Shiva, one of the Hindu trinity. The poem humorously depicts how the traditional "night-long Shiva wake," with its austere religious observances, has gradually devolved into a nocturnal celebration of modern day pop culture.

292
Sheila celebrated *Shiv Raathri*
staying up all night, watching
a three-part Telugu video
by the same name—
nine hours, all told.
Raised in the severe
Shivite Brahmin sect,
she has been observing
the Night of Shiva religiously,
except for the year of her Ninth Standard,
when she came down with Malaria.
The nocturnal affair falls on the
Great New Moon, each year.
Shiva, as gods go, is
a serious dude, as the
kids in Sheila's class might put it;
what with the cobra snakes,
skull-necklaces, and
crushing demons underfoot
in his dreaded Death Dance!
Shiva hangs out in the
cremation grounds,
a lean, mean, and

austere figure, meditating
amidst lowly goblins
and eerie draculas.
Shiva, AKA *Kaala Bhairav,*
who rides the big black dog,
is none other than
the very custodian of Time,
and all else that is relative!

293
Vijay, though a natural-born
Vaishnavite (a sect of
Brahmins who worship
not *Shiva*, but *Vishnu*,
the laid-back Lord),
had little choice but
stay up with Sheila, regardless.
Hinduism is a funny thing;
it's hilarious, actually!
They even sell colorful
comics on it, in Calcutta.
Hinduism is more of
an art form—an allegory really,
than a rulebook type religion;
it's very human,
and user-friendly;
you can take it, or
you can leave it,
these gods can handle it.
They have epics and operas,
temples and sculptures
dedicated to these
Aryan archetypes
of ancient Near Asia.

294
Vijay agreed to stay up,
but refused to watch the
video trash.
Instead, he started on
Brothers Karamazov,
put it aside
after a while,
and watched ESPN
in the kitchen.
They had on
an equestrian event:
attractive young women,
wearing ball caps,
coaxing their horses
over watery hurdles.
Vijay remembered Reeves,
the Superman, with a shudder.
Sheila made *Chaat* and *Samosas*;
bought *Barfi* and *Bobbattu*
from the Little India store.
They ate, they drank (oh, just tea and
Ovaltine!), roughing
the longest and darkest of nights!

Pediatric Pine Box Policy

Sheila doesn't quite know how to react when Tasha, her teaching assistant, shares with her the tragic practice of mothers of young black children buying special life insurance policies on their kids, just to be able to pay for their funeral expenses, in case they perish in street violence! This gives Sheila pause—she is overcome with doubt as to her role in the betterment of inner city children. She is surprised to see how the American experience is forcing changes within her.

295
Tasha was tidying up
the classroom, one
Friday afternoon.
Old workbooks,
paper, and gum wrappers
lay littered on the floor.
Sheila was poring over
publishers' catalogs,
looking for books
on parabolas and other
parametric palm sweaters.
Tasha broke the silence:
"I was listening to a report
on the radio, on how
some minority mothers
are drawing insurance policies
on their children, to be able
to pay for the kids' funerals,
just in case of a street shooting.

How much sadder can it get?
And what will they call it, the
Pediatric Pine Box Policy?"

296
Sheila looked at Tasha,
not knowing what to say.
The two have come to be
very close over the long
school year, now
drawing to a close.
Sheila realized she
has been thrust into the
middle of minority
struggles with Middle
America.
She was dabbling,
an outsider from the
other side of the world,
meddling with the minds
of beleaguered black children.
Kids struggling to find
a foothold in an unreceptive
world.
What gave her the
license, her math diploma?

297
Sheila was, most of all,
quizzical at herself.
She experienced a bout of
severe self-examination.
A South Indian *Hudigi*,
stepping into the middle

of the African American scene,
undertaking half-heroic measures
in the name of teaching math!
For their part,
Nalini and friends thought
Sheila was nuts.
Vijay corroborated
with formal diagnosis.
Sheila was hard on herself,
questioning, "Me, Miss Innovation?!"
She recalled
she was no more than
a fly on the wall,
back in India,
in the hot and dusty
Hoysala High.
And the whole music thing,
what drove her to do it?
Thank Thayappa, it worked!
"This America, I can't
believe it's changing me.
I'm no longer my
erstwhile mousy little
Sheila Murthy self!"

An Old Confluence Reunites: India and the West

Delves into the historical backdrop, mainly involving the British colonization of India, which resulted in the familiarization of Western culture with the Indians, especially the English language. This turns out to be a definite advantage for modern-day Indians as they aspire and prepare to come west, many of whom tend to skip over the UK, preferring to come to the US instead. The segment also sheds light on these relatively unique "prefab immigrants" from India and what makes them tick.

298
It's an Old Confluence
reuniting after a bend
in the river,
flowing over rocky gorges
and boulder-strewn bergschrunds;
a river of time and unlikely
confluence of cultures.
No, not like the green Alaknanda
and the blue Bhagirathi
merging naturally over
the heights of Dev Prayag.
Rather, picture the ice—
bergy bits and growlers—
of the alpine Rhine, turning East
and tumbling all the way
to the tropics, to the lower latitudes,
and melting into the tepid, faraway Kaaveri,
meandering, lost in meditation.

299
The Indies and the English
have always had a
bitter-sweet affair.
Even broken marriages
benefit from passage of
time and nurtured nostalgia.
The Mughals and their Taj,
later the English and their Raj;
clash of cultural plates,
all part of not so
remote a history.
Kipling's Hindustan
was the site
where imperialistic
impulses were humbled
by a half-naked man,
who was hell-bent for peace!

300
Dramatic developments
occurring daily, even hourly,
render stale the morning news,
what to say of last century's
Gandhi and his truth tactics…
A moral victory for the *Mahatma*
and his mobilized masses—true;
though not quite an innings defeat
for the monarchy!
Hardly a century later,
the field is unrecognizable.
The players and teams, and
the very pitch have altered.
It's not just cricket anymore.

The Indians today are
becoming proficient
at many games
people play, in the
new epicenter of existence,
which is the US of A!

301
Whoa, not so fast!
First, how did we get here?
What's the backstory?
The solid subcontinent that was India,
situated right in the middle of
East-West commerce,
was nevertheless isolated,
even insulated.
Indeed, it was meandering, lost in meditation,
allowing all and sundry
to go take a peek,
break an idol, or throw a rock.
Alexander the Great,
the marauding Moghuls, or
a traveling Oriental,
were all attracted to
this mystical mass of land—India.
But it was essentially
the Europeans, especially the English,
who were attracted to India,
like a moth to light!
It was like
they had everything back home,
except this India!
Just a sea voyage,
some ships, sails,

and brute force
was all it took for the crafty company
to take things over.
And, wow, did they like what they found!
So they made camp,
and, like, simply colonized!
They dug into the soft earth
and subjugated the passive people.
The English loved India
more than they hated it...
it's just not the boatloads of stuff
they carried back.
India helped the British discover themselves
and fine-tune their methods,
offering them a wider playing field
and suitably subdued subjects.
Sure, there was much ambivalence,
because the British were a fair-minded,
not so fair a people,
if you know what I mean!
They sent in
brutes-in-military-boots, true;
but they also sent Patrician
professors and statesmen—
men who were thoughtful,
sensitive, even kind.
These men saw more
than diamonds and spices,
they found a people,
and a special civilization.
All this makes for ambivalence,
which still hangs in the air...
in nearby Blair and everywhere.

302
But forget history,
just for a moment,
and forgive the players,
for they've all passed on...
What isn't clear is
what's with these modern day
"prefab immigrants," who are
dubbed the Model Minority—these
caricatures of the curry culture?
They sure make
for a masala migrant story!

303
From the land of bustling
bazaars and buffalo chips,
these sons and daughters
of India, descend into
the valley of Silicon chips.
Their minds naturally
attuned to math, and studies
heavily geared to science,
these nerdy, none-too-
hardy stick figures
come to the aid
of a self-indulgent society,
malnourished, poised
for fresh legs.
They're rediscovering
America, long and after
Louis & Clark, thanking
Company Boeing
for the rather easy going.

304
It's amazing how it works.
They come in, plug in,
and *voila'*, the light comes on!
Instant immigration—
from a rubbish heap
to the top, in one leap!
These East Indies have
arrived quietly,
yet count among
the top wage earners.
They're the scientists,
engineers, and doctors,
businessmen, and entrepreneurs;
they're the drained brains
from distant shores,
the latest transatlantic transplants!
305
The secret of their success?
An ancient Indian recipe,
like *Aaloo Gobhi*.
Education, education, *and*
education!
Feed them
math formula in skimmed
buttermilk!
Hit'em on
the head with books,
early, like age-three.
Teach them to recite
tongue-twisting stanzas
in ancient *Sanskrit*.
(Never mind the meaning,
it's the memory, stupid!)

Questioning and reasoning,
keep it for later.
Cram their
little RAMs with stories and fables,
and quiz them to death!

306
These Indies, they may not be the brightest,
but,
they're able and stable.
High Funda, *yaar!*
You'd better be, otherwise,
in a land of a billion-plus,
you'll be swept off your *chappals*!
For instance, the India class
of any given year is in the millions!
You learn to find your place
in the teeming masses;
also lessons of patience
and inner-discipline.
On the appointed day,
you land at JFK—
it's a piece of cake—really!

The Bhaskars are Bullish on America!

Like many of today's immigrant professionals from India, Vijay and Sheila have few complaints, actually, "they are having a ball in the US of A!" They love their jobs and are amazed by the power of the dollar, which allows them to purchase many material goods. The reader is taken along on a shopping expedition to the local mall on a Saturday morning.

307
The Bhaskars, if it's not
amply clear, are
enjoying the heck out of America!
To their great surprise,
it's the jobs—mere meal tickets
back home in *Bharath*—which
are tapping dormant, heretofore
unused outlets in them.
They love the clear-cut
assignments they both are
presented at their respective
jobs.
Even more, they love
the workers' independence,
daunting at first, intoxicating
once you get the hang of it.
You're commissioned with,
placed in charge of, directing
another human being,
an American, no less!

308
Our guest workers like the
prompt feedback they receive,
on the efficacy of
their endeavors.
If your
work is good, the word is
spread through the neighborhood.
If not, they don't exactly
roll your head, they send
you back to Driver's Ed!
You receive your paycheck
by month's end, barring the
world's very end, often carrying
a dandy dividend.
The work-a-day world
of America, it keeps
you productive, even if it
becomes highly addictive!

309
Pertaining to the paycheck,
we're talking US dollars!
You don't have to be a
Tenth Grade math teacher
from that hot and dusty land
a few laps from *Laksha Dweep*,
to know that a dollar is
many multiple
times the value of the rueful
Indian *Rupee*.
Right there,
dear reader, is the difference
two worlds make!

If the dollar equals, say,
seventy rupees, then, is one
arbitrary American equal to
the same number of indigent Indians?
Morbid math for sure, but
isn't it kinda how it is?

310
"The cool part is the buying
power of the dollar,"
cooed Sheila, thumbing through
discount catalogs.
"If you factor in the
purchasing power of the
Green Back, and keep in mind
the cut-throat contrast in terms
of the exchange value,
my calculation shows
that on a given workday,
the dollared, stiff-collared
worker, by lunch time, earns
what the average *Deshi*
earns in a month!"

311
Sheila, a thrifty maid by
nature as by nurture,
loves to lock her dollars
with tellers, wearing pastel
colors.
She commandeers
the Correctional check,
as soon as Vijay brings it home.
'Saved money spells security,

and frugal ways furnish
the future' are her driving
dictums—dicta, if you wish!
Thus, our math-minded minstrel,
one can be sure, is no wastrel.
Her heart stops several times
a day, when she sees things
she would salvage, are tossed
casually into the garbage.
"It would do them good to go
without food, for a day or two!"
she would fume.

312
Yet still, the magic of the
American marketplace
uncurls the tightest fist.
Sheila is overwhelmed
by the sheer range of choices,
even more by the price of goods!
They snare you out of the
suburbs on Saturday
mornings, hawking "everything's
eighty-percent off!"
Sheila shamelessly frequents
bottom line boutiques, such as
Bang-4-UR-Buck, or
Dollar-R-Our-Molar.
She attacks the aisles
assiduously,
looking for brand-name bargains,
dirt-cheap even
by *Dravidian* standards.

313
Sheila would rouse
Vijay out of bed
saying "it's 9 o'clock!"
having already showered and sung
her Saturday *Sanskrit sthothrams*.
After *idli, saambar*,
and Instant Nescafe,
they ride in their Japanese sedan,
duly seat-belted and driving defensively.
At the Madison Avenue Mall,
Sheila joins her friend Nalini,
who's waiting by the
One Hour Photo booth.
The two pair off, on a mission of
calculated consumerism.
Vijay, bereft of his better half,
summons sufficient cheer
and heads to, where else
but Barnes & Noble!

314
A brightly lit bookstore
open 24x7,
spacious, speckled with
hostesses, ever so gracious.
From A for Amazon, to
Z for Zeitgeist, they carry
every printed letter and word.
Books are to B & N,
what booze is to a bootlegger.
Vijay, a baptized bibliophile,
felt particularly noble,
palming the silky best sellers
in the vast Barnes' stable.

He ordered a half-caf and
coffee cake,
at the Starbucks-by-the-books.

315
America, you truly are a miracle!
You're indeed the land
of milk and honey,
excessively successful
and enterprising
with a capital E.
You cater to all tastes,
and serve a hundred tongues.
No one is neglected,
nor excessively vexed,
not even those who
slack up on your rules.
You're big, and you're strong,
from the Oregon-on-the-Pacific
to the majestic Maine,
shining like that Western Star,
your larger-than-life John Wayne!
If individual spirits shrivel
and brook bigotry,
they're simply outside the pale
of your magnanimous mission.

316
Coffee and cake
have a way of adding to
Vijay's already effulgent spirit.
Ensconced in a polished highchair,
a wooden throne smack in the middle
of Middle America,
the part-time prisoner

is particularly relishing the moment.
It's easy to be in awe
of this place they call America—
for what's there to complain?
Still, Vijay chuckled to himself
(from behind the covers of a
book on cat-lovers), thinking
of one newly arrived
Bangarappa from ChikBallapur,
whose only complaint
was that there are far
too many Americans in America!

317
While Vijay was thus
wistfully wasteful, exercising
his guaranteed freedoms,
his Bangalorean bride,
in the company of Nalini,
another exquisite-looking
expatriate, was busy
walking through Walmart.
"Look at these fluffy, soft,
pillows for two dollars!"
exclaimed Sheila.
"Have you
seen this Teflon frying pan?
Ideal for making *dosa*—
yours for five bucks!"
chimed in her chum.
They walk through toys,
towels, and toilet bowls,
past cordless phones,
through stuff affordable
American dreams are made of…

Like a Bandy-legged Bengali Boatman

It's the last day of school at MLK High, and graduation day is coming up. Mr. Moody, the principal, is pleased with the success of the graduating class whom "he has guided to the far bank and deposited them on dry land." The segment also describes a special luncheon given on the university campus in honor of Sheila and Tasha by college volunteers who had the opportunity to serve Sheila's tenth-grade class at MLK High.

318
Last day of school, at MLK High.
The kids are on a drug-free high,
as the teachers let out
a long-held sigh.
Candid colors and loosely held
fashions, at Mr. Moody's
assembly.
He demanded
attention—didn't get it.
The kids smiled, he smiled back.
Abandoning the American
tradition of the Prepared
Speech, Mr. Moody made
the rounds of the
Senior Class,
who would be graduating
the following weekend.
He hugged the giddy girls
with gusto, and high-fived

the boys.
He's guided
them to the far bank,
like a Bandy-legged
Bengali boatman,
and deposited them
on dry land.
319
The college kids, who have
collaborated with Sheila
and Tasha over the long
school year, invited the two
to lunch at the university.
Aaron was instrumental
in securing select seats
in the Garden Café.
The math and music majors,
some with their dogs, others
with guitars, welcomed the
pretty pedagogicians.
Members of the college
chess club, reduced to
mere pawns in the hands
of the two live queens,
were also in attendance.
They dined on garden salad,
dressed with lemon *tahini,*
pimento cheese sandwiches,
crunchy blue-corn chips,
and the Garden Café
special Gazpacho soup!

Hungry Men in Dungarees

A short, satirical tale of "serial snatchings"
from the prison kitchen.

320
Vijay was called to witness
a prosecution, in the case of
The hungry inmate versus
the well-fed People of the county.
It was alleged that Joe Blow
stole some mustard,
found on his person
when patted down.
The prison court met
in the chow hall,
the supposed scene of
serial snatchings of
controlled condiments
and forbidden foodstuffs,
perpetrated by a gang of
hungry men in dungarees!

321
The court was called to order
by Mr. Mike Murchison,
known to doomed defendants
as Maximum Murchison.
"They say you took some
mustard from the kitchen.
How do you plead?"
demanded Murchison
cutting the crime to the chase.
Joe Blow blanched, looked up

at the prison prosecutor,
whose face remained
unflinched, clenched, and locked shut.
'No loquacious logic
would cut mustard,
not with this fellow' reasoned Blow,
deciding, for once, to tell the truth.
"Well, it's true I stoled the mustard,
but that's because I was hungry!"
"That'll do. You plead guilty—
seven days in solitary!"
Murchison marched on.

In the Clutches of a Culture Vulture

This is a lengthy, often humorous segment about Vijay and Sheila's vacation to the North East. In New York city, they are joined by Dr. Anand, the cultural anthropologist (and Sheila's second cousin) who tours them around the city and later drives them up to Niagara Falls and back. The talkative professor takes advantage of his "car seat captives" and expounds freely on Americans and their unique culture.

322
Vijay and Sheila weasel
a few days of vacation,
and venture out on
a low-cost excursion
to the tourist treadmills
on the Eastern Seaboard.
"Niagara is a must—
do see it from the Canadian side!"
insisted Indira, a friend of Nalini.
Of course, thought Sheila,
who's had her eye on the Falls
ever since she changed
over to *salwars*.
First stop: Washington, D.C.,
the Superpower seat.
Next, on to the Big Apple,
now bruised somewhat.

323
They flew Etna Airlines,
which offered cheap fares,
before it would erupt and
go bankrupt.
Sheila packed two suitcases,
carefully cushioning the silks
from Vijay's *Sholapuri* slippers,
and savage baggage handlers.
She managed a few winks
and woke up to find Vijay
soundly asleep.
The ever-agreeable and equanimous Accord,
a proven ground transport,
got them to the airport.
Levies, lines, and fines,
as anticipated; checkers
and stickers later,
they are duly seated.
She got the window
and Vijay is sandwiched, as usual.

324
The politics of power—
of the people, by the people,
for the people—are played out daily,
on the banks of the placid,
nonpartisan Potomac.
None less than the leader
of the Free World resides here!
Lives are legislated;
liberties are litigated,
if not ligated;
government agents go

about their cloak & dagger
routines, clad barely in
bullet-proof vests.
Vijay and Sheila arrive in
Cherry Tree George's layout,
on a gorgeous summer day-out!

325
Day One was dedicated to
monuments and mausoleums.
Lincoln's Log Cabin legend
is more familiar to the
average South Indian,
than the genius of Jefferson.
They stand in line,
and take flash photos
of the patriarchs and protagonists
of the off-Broadway spoof,
Founding Dads.
A tall monument
perhaps to the patience
of the patriotic people
waiting in line, they ride
the symbolic *Shiv Ling*
to its pinnacle, the view
coming as a climax
to their first fun-filled day!

326
The musty Municipal Museum
of the erstwhile *Mulligatawny* Madras,
Sheila's only prior contact
with dusty, decaying artifacts,
was hardly preparation enough.

The series of museums
called the Smithsonian
simply arrested and awe-inspired
our logarithmist from *Lal Bagh*.
Vijay was partial to Aerospace,
while Sheila wanted to stick
around Art and Natural History.
They walked and gawked
all day, until lights out.

327
Sheila's second cousin, Anand,
(the long-winded NYU anthropologist—
surely, you recall!)
received them at Kennedy.
Vijay was ambivalent,
at best, remembering
the assistant professor's
addiction to unchecked oration.
Yet still, it's unthinkable to tour
the city without a dependable *Deshi*—
for a guide, happy host, and chauffeur—
a normal Indian practice.
Still, four days with
Dr. Bipolar, in a beat up,
bitty Buick Coupe?!
"*Howdappa*, how can you forget
life's a package deal?" Sheila
inquisitioned.
"*Howdu, Thaayi, howdu...*"
Vijay ruefully receded.

328
The academician bachelor's abode
was itself of anthropologic interest,

Vijay noted to himself.
The hole-in-the-Manhattan-wall
was like a philosopher's pig sty.
Books, papers, and periodicals
were strewn all over
the threadbare carpet;
Baroque batik bed sheets
barely covered the box springs;
discs and dust covers served
as stepping stones
to a tentative kitchen
and hopeful tenure.
"This guy's badly in
need of a wife!" exclaimed Sheila,
secretly thinking of Pramitha,
cousin Prathima's friend,
as a possible candidate.

329
From surface transport
they transferred to the
subway—back and forth, all day.
Anand was an artful aficionado
of the underground system,
used to diving in and out,
and dodging crowds.
Sheila held on to her purse
and bodily possessions,
wary of jewel thieves and
passing perverts.
"When they take you for an
out-of-towner, they really
take you!" Anand teased,
himself deriving perverse pleasure.

They walked Wall Street,
gaping at the trading houses
of the world's free markets.
A casual mention of Madison Avenue
and the commercial ad-ventures thereof,
had to do.
Lower Manhattan, Upper East Side,
richer Westchester, poorer Harlem,
Bohemian Brooklyn, and
the beastie Bronx Zoo—
were all shown with copious commentary.
They drove past Skid Row,
Tin Pan Alley, and the
five-hundred flags over
the United Nations.
They passed up the
Tourist steamer and a ride
to the top of the Empire State,
now restored to its previous place
as the city's tallest structure—
lonely, but still standing.

330
The next day, after breakfast
at a *Oothappam* and
Upma joint in Jackson Heights,
they walked through a series
of sari and spice shops,
making perfunctory
perambulations of all things Indian.
On the highway to Niagara,
Dr. Anand deconstructs
America as a capricious
concept, contrasting it

to its headwaters in Europe.
Vijay has had his fill
of the Culture Vulture's
categorical commentaries,
and develops a
classic case of a captive's
Learned Helplessness Response.
He tarries longer and
longer at each gas stop,
adopting unabashed
toilet-stalling tactics!

331
Motion sickness, monotonous
monologues after,
the vaunted waters
were finally at hand.
Once upon a time
there was a river,
which the native peoples
named Niagara.
Their own time has come and gone,
and the river moved on.
It's now the tourists,
touts, and traffic cops,
who flock to its banks—
pardon the pun.
Anand arranged a rash
vortexual voyage, into
the eddies and currents,
and bounding buckets
of the great falls.
Sheila, shrieking with delight
like a sixth grader, gets wet,
defeating her yellow coveralls.

332
The girl from the
land of the great *Ganges*,
which issues from the
matted dreads of the
severe *Shiva's* skull-strong head,
makes contact with the holy
molecules, not along
the burning banks of the
beggar-ridden Benares,
but here, in New York state's Niagara!
What Benares, what New York,
before *Shiva Shakti's*
shake, rattle, and roll
of this world,
nay, the entire Creation,
dissolving time, terrain,
and the very storyline!
Millennia pass like minutes;
Man and his mundane
peeves and petitions melt away,
carried by the rapid torrents
and ravages of time!

333
Anand had one more ace
up his sleeve.
On the penultimate day of
their nor'easter,
he dragged our tired tourists
through many toll booths,
tailgating the traffic
in his battered Buick—where to?
To the lovely Longwood Gardens,

in DuPont's Delaware.
Sheila, and more so, Vijay,
still skeptical of their host's
tastes and travel tactics,
proceeded without protest
into the pristine park.
"Oh, my God, Vijju, *eshtu
chennagide, nodu!*"
Sheila exulted abruptly.
The flowers and trees
wreaked their magic
on the unsuspecting outlanders,
just as their clever
culture coach had wagered.

334
Actually, Anand's ploy
exceeded expectations,
and worked to perfection.
Vijay's palpable reticence
and passive resistance
quickly evaporated.
He was simply floored
by the fabulous flora.
Longwood's gigantic trees,
representing every genus
and species, laid out artfully
along leisurely avenues
and boulevards,
reminded him of Bangalore's *Lal Bagh*—
which, however, was no match
for this green and serene preserve.
With its ferns and flower galleries,
inside carefully cultivated green houses,

Longwood was very enchanting.
Sheila was particularly
taken in by the baby-sized
Bonsais, bearing witness to
the Orientalists' subtle
spirit and balance.

335
After days of being held as
a car seat captive,
the prison psychologist had
to simply vent.
"You keep saying how clever
and capable these whites are,"
said Vijay, addressing his
comments to Anand,
the white-people worshipper.
"I'll give it to you—
they're that and more.
Take this garden,
for instance; a misnomer
for what's a piece of paradise!
Sure, those giant trees grew on
their own; but behind it all,
you see an intelligent, *human* hand.
What care, what s*hraddha,*
westerners show in doing things...
Just looking at their handiwork—
call me a pushover—
the white civilization is where it's at!"
waxed Vijay, going
a bit over the top.

261

Vijay Receives the Callow Client

This is a continuation of Rashad Richardson's rather serious saga from the previous segments. Vijay, the prison psychologist, is finally able to see Rashad in his office after the latter relents and opens up emotionally. The fifteen-year-old is quite lost in the adult prison, faced with long years of incarceration ahead of him. He is thrown into the midst of experienced convicts as punishment for the murder of his father.

336
"It's like that from the git-go.
Daddy was the Big Dog,
and our mother, a docile
doormat.
As a kid, I didn't
think much about it,
it all seemed so natural.
Besides, mom never complained,
told him off, or anything
like that.
Looking back,
I guess she was scared
that had she said something,
daddy would go apeshit
and we might all get beat!
Until it happened, um,
until I shot him,
I never realized
what I was carrying

inside of me;
That I hated his very
sight, even though he
wasn't messing with me,"
read Rashad's letter to Dr. Bhaskar.

337
Vijay processed the
four-page prison parchment,
written in typical
schoolboy scrawl.
He certainly took
his time, Rashad Richardson did,
to open up and
share with the world
why he shot and
killed the big Bull Dog.
What Rashad didn't
realize was—you can't
kill a family pet,
no matter how vicious the pit bull got.
They've got Leash Laws,
Cruelty Crusaders,
Least Restrictive Clauses,
and all that—call it
the English Canine Law.
The kid did what he
had to do; in the process,
he ran up against
a mendacious, middle-class mindset.

338
Now that the youth allowed
him a foot in the door,

what's the Paid Pacifier
to do?
Collaborate with
the kid, in rationalizing
away the situation?
That life sucked, anyway?
Especially, for his kind
of people?
That sooner or later,
all his cousins and homies
are also headed for prison?
No, Vijay is not there;
not quite into
the Whatever-Works-Workbook.
Instead, he will have to
nurture hope against hope;
and teach the boy
Active Acceptance,
no matter he's frigging fifteen...

339
Rashad is rounded up
and brought into the clinic.
He's a scrawny, gangling lad,
with adolescent awkwardness
written all over.
He looks anything but
dangerous, which makes
a mockery of the metal chains
and the macho escort.
A wounded bird, out of its
element, uncomfortable,
and avoiding a well-meaning
human hand.

Vijay comes out of his office
to receive the callow client,
earmarked for special
dispensation; courtesy:
MLK High Tenth Grade
Teachers Association.

340
Rashad was somewhat
reserved and reticent;
Vijay, very supportive
and facilitative.
(Time for Unconditional Positive Regard—
per Carl the Compassionate's canon, Vijay
realized.)
Vijay was able to
establish that the kid
was still in one piece;
eating and sleeping mostly,
like an inchoate embryo,
still in the first trimester.
He praised the youth
for surviving the shock of
the first three months,
saying he'll soon
be delivered
from the toughest part—
the toughest part
of a very great fall;
like jumping from
a plane in full flight,
and not knowing the ropes.

341
Back in the dorm,
they soothe him:
"It will come to you,
not to worry."
"It's a long fall; you'll
hit the ground, when
you hit the ground!"
the old cons advise Rashad.
"Worryin' about it only
makes it worser" they say,
saying the obvious.
The mongrel, motley
men in their mid-forties,
gather around the
cowering cub, urging him:
"Meanwhile, tap your peeps
for some tobacco money!"

Sheila Attends the Summer Math Institute

The long segment begins with a refreshing personal experience for Sheila, which she shares with her close friend and fellow immigrant Nalini, throwing in her insights and social/cultural observations about Americans and their culture. The poem then lapses further into a stark contrast between the temperaments of Westerners and Easterners, focusing more on the people of India, who are shaped by their markedly overpopulated country, where a surprising number still survive, even succeed.

342
Sheila's summer hols
were enjoyable,
mainly for the decadent,
domestic languor.
Mindless masala videos, and
long pointless phone calls
to any and every
homebound handset-holder
made up her days,
until invited to attend
the Summer Math Institute
for secondary school teachers.
Sheila wasn't crazy about going,
but as a die-hard *Dakshin Khand*
achiever, she couldn't
pass up the Learning Op.

343
The university math department
was organizing the institute,
meant for planners and specialists
in mathematical education.
Sheila's name was included
by Ms. Roxanna Roberson
from the Central Office,
who was also attending.
Dean Broadhead came in
briefly and declared the
session open. The two-week
training took off, when
Professor Peter Pratt
took over. Wasting little time,
they formed various work
groups, focusing on
Elementary, Middle, and
High School teaching needs.

344
Sheila was teamed with
teachers from two
private high schools,
who were friendly
and focused on
the task at hand.
Sheila noticed that
her group was all white,
except for a man,
the only one, who
hailed from Ecuador.
They worked on
various issues:

making math seem
more relevant;
non-traditional teaching
approaches, integrating
science and basic math,
advanced track instruction
for acute math minds, etc.
Sheila soaked up the
ideas, like a spongy *Rosgolla*
soaked in rose-scented syrup!

345
Group work brought them
closer, as the days progressed.
Robin, who emerged as the
undeclared team leader,
showed much interest in
Sheila and her cultural
background. A pro, by now,
Sheila anticipated the
deferentially framed
delvings into The
Encyclopedia Indica:
The Red Dot, Arranged Marriage,
and, of course, the Holy Cow.
Robin, to her credit, was
not completely clueless.
She has heard of Ravi Shankar,
and his silver-stringed *Sitar*.
She loved the Indian cuisine:
"what do they call it,
Chicken Tikka Masala? Yum!"

346
"The Americans are so sincere,
and so respectful to us,
it's touching,"
Sheila conveyed to Nalini,
during their post-potato roast
phone chat. "Now, I'm
developing a similar
respect towards the
Americans, myself!
I know, you know this:
Growing up, I never felt
true respect for many of our
people back home, in India.
I mean, I didn't much care
for my colleagues, teachers,
or professors there.
Most seemed so conceited
and self-serving,
some, even callous.
But not these Americans,
who're so—what's the word—
earnest!" Sheila said,
rather earnestly.

347
Sense and sensibility are
shaped by centuries of
shared living, in zones
of comfort. The Europeans
and their descendants
tend to be restrained,
and fairly reserved,
though the odd Italian

may be the exception.
These strong, silent,
stiff-upper-lippers,
famous for their scaled down
speech and euphonic euphemisms,
mostly carry self-effacing
and dispassionate profiles,
all the while concealing
active minds—"just conserving
a whiff of oxygen, thank you!"

348
Whereas, the cultural
caricature of a South Indian,
is quite the contrary:
loud and long-winded,
grabbing and bragging,
calculating and
too clever by a half;
these under-exercised bodies
and overheated minds
from the tropics, though
seasoned survivalists, they're
lost in these cold-water ports,
choking on an excess
baggage of cynicism.
Let's do the math, on India.
A billion anything is
a thousand millions.
Imagine a thousand million
humans, where the Maximum
Operating Capacity is three hundred mils!
Too close for comfort?
"Yeah, a bit over the top,"

an understated Oregonian might concede.
It's a prescription for pandemonium,
what to say of cynicism.
Hypotheses get tested,
and egos get testy,
as the one interacts with
a thousand others,
in a matter of hours!
You'll likely meet
a dozen imbeciles,
and as many geniuses,
on a given day.
You get seasoned, stir-fried,
and processed into
a peevish people person!

349
Beyond a certain number,
any bureaucracy
simply breaks down,
as is the case in India.
The country itself turns
into a billion-man boondoggle.
Deep-seated despair spreads,
and people are left to
their own devices.
That's when the human
spirit flourishes, as there's
nowhere to go, but up!
An ancient society can
accommodate adversity.
It falls back on its best
and only resource—
people—plenty of them!

Education and enterprise
become the twin mantras,
as the cream rises to the
top and spills out of
the country, making room
for reams of fresh dreams.

350
Still speaking of India,
advantages are bestowed,
not just on aristocrats,
but all able and willing cats.
The Silver Spoon birth
is no myth; yet, alternate routes
are there for those who
can fly below the radar.
Education and enterprise,
do lead to good jobs and
do open gates;
not just in America,
but globally, all over.
In a crowded field containing
innumerable Indians,
it's those with guts and
gumption, accolades and
high ambition, who win.
Sure, caste and creed still carry
pull and confer connections,
otherwise unavailable to
the unaccounted masses.

Recovered Memories

A tragic and unfortunate story about a runaway child from the South who ends up living in San Francisco. Years later, his return to the South is once again marred by untoward events. The story does not quite end there...

351
If enough negatives pile up,
you too will do the unthinkable.
Take the case of
Grandy Grissom, from the
all-time classics of CCC.
An early morning fog
in the Carolina hills,
curtailed more than visibility,
as the multi-car pile-up
entailed many lives,
on that fateful day.
The young and hopeful Grissoms,
with their two kids
in the back of their
family-friendly van,
were counted among
the massive casualties.
Somehow, our four-year-old
Grandy was spared—
spared to live a life of trauma,
he now says sardonically.
His extended family
took in Grandy, along with
the all-but-totalled van;

and, in the name of discipline
and the divine, totalled
the boy's bouncy spirit and
innate good nature.
It was a different kind
of pile-up, as Grandy sees it.

352
Starved for love,
and suffocated by stoicism
and sermons on self-control,
one day, the kid just took off.
Grissom was but nine,
when he ran from home.
He hitchhiked West,
washing the rigs during
the day, and riding
the trucks by night.
Unable to find a treehouse
or a traveling circus,
he settled for a
crack house in the city of Frisco.
The caretakers at the
crack house were compassionate
towards the stray kitten—
a babe too young for their
bathhouses and barbiturates.
To trust or not to trust,
was the question
for young Grandy, while
dealing with the rowdy,
rollicking, gay folk.
Luckily, they were loving and
considerate, without the
rustic rancor he ran from.

Our twisted Oliver grew up
in the fog and billowing
clouds of the Bay Area,
watching the Giants and
crisscrossing the Golden Gate;
an urban hiker in
shiny leather, who rode
a Harley and loved cold barley.

353
On a rare trip down south
he made with a biker
buddy from Brevard, NC,
Grissom encountered trouble.
He paid for his nonchalance,
and neurotic nostalgia for
his none-too-happy boyhood.
He ran into a hooligan,
a bike-riding bisexual,
who lacked finesse
and who forced the issue.
Grissom gagged before
he pulled out his gun,
and shot the ruffian
twice in the head.
Grissom was thus
rudely reunited
with his Recovered Memories.

354
Vijay was late coming into
this story, not before
one more murder
was committed by
the troubled tire-rider.

Grissom was guarded in
the session with Vijay,
who never met anyone
who killed twice.
There was a detectable
pattern to the killings:
both involved sex.
Vijay wasn't particularly
trained to work with
murderers, which called
for a forensic focus;
but he was at ease
with all humans even
if they had killed
other humans. Vijay
thus began conversing
with Grissom, like he would
with any man who had
occasion to repeat a feat.

355
Grissom, who was city-bred
and used to ethnic variety,
was able to discern the
Indian doctor's direct
approach, devoid of
professional artifice.
He decided to share
his life story with the
earnest-seeming Easterner.
"I had it rough
from the very start—
you might have read my file.
Mom and Dad were replaced
by some others in the family. Their

moralization and
mystification messed me up,
to put it starkly.
I had to leave—
I fled to the other coast,
finding compassion on the road,
sadly missing in my own abode."

356
"San Francisco, after
North Carolina, was a
whole 'nother world.
The big city
on the hill overlooking
the bay, its people marched
to a different drummer.
I ended up with the
more raunchy crowd,
and learned their
radical ways, rife with
repressed anger as I was.
In what's a pitiful irony,
I went on and befriended
the gay community,
which took me in as
a child and sheltered me.
I was picky in choosing
my partners, avoiding any
hint of aggression or
authoritarian tone."

357
"You're probably aware
of the rest. I had to kill this
guy who came on strong.

I was convicted of
Murder–Second Degree
and put in prison.
The story, however, is
not over. I became depressed
and tried to kill myself—
I drank some bleaching
agent, which didn't
quite finish me.
I was lying in a
hospital bed, in the
forensic ward.
There was this old man
in the bed next to mine.
He looked like he was
pushing his 70s.
Just my luck that
he turned out
to be a pedophile,
who was given to bragging
about his sordid seductions
of six-year-olds."

358
"I put him on notice
to stop talking about
the subject. But he was
a sicko, who wouldn't listen.
It was clear that he
was getting aroused
sharing the shameful
stories with me, as much
as he did from the
depraved deeds themselves.
He didn't realize

he was defiling me all
over again, each time he
mentioned his debaucheries.
It was more than I could take.
I got up and smothered
the sick son of a bitch
with a starched white
Hospital Pillow, until
he could breathe no more."

359
The session over, the
Californian returned to
the doom of doing time,
Vijay shut the door, to
cogitate and assimilate.
What sad stories!
Another severed spirit;
the fault lines grow only wider,
as the person gets older;
the damage can't be
undone, fait accompli—
it's done happened!
The rules are different for
the Little League—two strikes
and you're out; for life;
unless the baby formula,
and booster shots of love
and long-term coaching
are administered.
Dr. Bhaskar skipped lunch
and went on a long walk.

In a Muddy Little Ditch in the Middle of California!

Rajni and Ramakanth, friends of Vijay and Sheila, narrate their 1970s adventure to San Francisco and the Bay Area. The hilarious tale highlights the cultural challenges experienced by the visitors from Southern India as they tour bohemian Northern California in the '70s.

360
Rajni, wife of Ramakanth,
and Uma's mom, recounted
a story from the late seventies.
They were gathered in
the downstairs den, having
imbibed exquisite *Konkan*
fare, with little room to spare.
Over Ramakanth's polite protests,
which only reinforced Rajni to
proceed with greater flair,
she began:
"I want to tell you about our trip to
California, when we
visited San Francisco."

361
"Uma was but four, and Rama
had a conference,
for an excuse.
We stayed at the Four Seasons,
located in the middle of
the city—a grand affair;
thank goodness, the bill, we didn't

281

have to defray! Anyway,
Uma and I'd stay back
in the hotel watching TV,
until Rama was able to
cut out of the conference,
and we'd all go out
sightseeing: the Fisherman's
Wharf, Telegraph Hill, Chinatown,
the Japanese Stone Garden,
and, of course, Lombardi Street.
Oh yes, the San Francisco
Zoo, which Uma so enjoyed!"

362
"All this was fine, and I
highly recommend it
to the new arrivals here.
Our schedule in the
city over, we had plans
to visit my friend Delilah,
and her, how to put it,
her live-in friend, Dirk."
Dirk and Delilah (that's
her real name!) were
living in a bohemian
village, overlooking the bay
in Marin County, home of
the magnificent Muir Woods.
For us, it started like
'Three Little Indians
Visit the Tall Redwoods'."

363
"But something funny happened
on the way to the farm,

so to speak! I have to
tell you about D and D,
for you to better appreciate
this titillating tale.
Delilah is a tall, rangy
woman, blonde, beautiful, and
bold. She taught in Ivy League,
being a specialist in Classics
and Romance languages.
She was a poster child for
the then stormy feminist movement.
I met her at one of the yoga
classes I used to teach."

364
"Dirk, on the other hand,
was no novice—he was the
most adept *Hatha Yogi*
I had ever seen. The darkly
handsome Dirk was
also a feverish thinker,
writer, and philosopher,
a la Jiddu Krishnamurthy.
Together, Dirk and Delilah
fled civilization as we
knew it, choosing to hide
with the hippies in the hills.
Speaking of hills, Ramakanth
still rues that day when
he had to drive over those
hills in the dark, in a rental
car to boot!
Neither of us being naturals
at night navigation, and
having to first negotiate

the Golden Gate Bridge,
Ayyo deva, God knows, it was rough!"

365
"At last, we reached the place—
Molinas or Bolinas, some
such name. Their house on
the mesa afforded the most
majestic views—mountain
or metro—you can envision.
You sit on the deck all day,
and watch the gulls and
pelicans dive into the bay!
Delilah was down-to-earth
and friendly, while Dirk
engaged Ramakanth in
philosophical jivegressions."

366
"After lunch, it being a summer day,
D and D suggested we all
go for a dip in a nearby
pond or lake. Uma brought
out her little swimsuit,
while Dirk lent Rama
a pair of his shorts;
I wore the *sari*, as always;
thus, we set out.
It was a short drive, in their
VW Microbus. We disembarked
from the bohemian bus,
and blinked in the bright sunshine.
Uma started walking ahead
of us, towards what she thought
was a suburban swimming pool."

367
"Both Delilah and Dirk remained cool
as Culver City cucumbers, and
the two of us casually ambled along.
Lo and behold,
I never saw anything like that
in my born days—young men and
women, completely naked!
I'll let my husband tell you
what all happened next,
because I closed my eyes
and simply disappeared
into the woods!"
Rajni stopped, and Ramakanth
laughingly continued:
"Really, it was simply shocking to
see so many people in a
small area, without any clothes on!"

368
"There was this Muddy Little Ditch
with hardly any water, into
which young fellows in the buff
were Tarzan-swinging from the trees!
Young men and women were
sprawled naked on the grass,
lying next to each other,
taking in the sun.
Where would you look, which way
would you turn?!
Uma, who was too young
to know what's going on,
was enjoying herself
making friends;

and Rajni—she was
nowhere to be seen!"

369
"Left alone, I kept close
to Delilah, who abruptly
removed her clothes,
right in front of me!
I, then, ran to this fellow Dirk,
our *Hatha Yogi*, who, with equal
agility, doffed his drawers
and assumed the Lotus pose—
sitting on his bottom,
pink as a rose!"

370
"The bizarre behavior of
our host and hostess,
let alone the perverted public,
put me in a hopeless situation.
I felt naked and totally exposed,
standing there still shod in
my borrowed blue shorts,
while no one else had a
stitch of cloth on them!
I had no choice but seek
refuge in the shallow pool;
and sit down in the silt
and mud, just to conceal
my offending knickerbockers
from plain view of the
nude Nature Lovers!"

371
"That's when this older man,
suitably shriveled, came
wading towards me,
with his hands clasped
in the Indian-style greeting.
He said, '*Namasthe, Rama*!'
which further shocked me—
'he even knows my name!'
Of course, he didn't.
He went on to introduce
his beautiful bare-naked wife,
and their pot-puffing
pre-pubescent son—both
standing on the beleaguered banks,
their fair skin glistening
in the afternoon sun..."

372
"You go where life takes you;
even if it is a mudhole,
in the middle of
majestic California!
Who knew beautiful-babes-
in-the-buff, every bit as
sexy and seductive as
Adam's Eve, would one day
drive me into a ditch and
out of my mind?!
Looking back,
my problem was
this thing called Cool,
we Indians utterly lack!
Still, for our host

and hostess to leave me
in the lurch, thus
forcing me into that ditch,
why, I'll never forgive!"

373
"The communal bath over,
our hosts took us back home,
where we were allowed
time to recoup.
That evening, Dirk treated
me to a lecture on the
need for hallucinogens,
in tandem with *Hatha Yoga*,
in order to gain Full Realization.
When he found out that I was
closer to a *Bhogi* than a *Yogi*,
he insisted that I try smoking pot.
Believe it or not, I hardly took
a drag on the funny-smelling
cigarette, when I started
giggling uncontrollably, while
Rajni didn't see what's funny!"
374
"We got out of there the next
morning, having had a most
memorable holiday. We heard
of California being special
and unique, but never dreamt
that it would be so nutty!
We're still in touch with Delilah
and Dirk, two highly individualistic
Californians. I'm afraid
we Indians know nothing,

besides the Nine-to-Five.
There's so much we can learn
from these adventurous Americans.
No, I am not preaching we all get
naked and smoke marijuana,
but we could be more daring,
more *alive*. Nothing like an
educated, enlightened American,
who's open-minded
and willing to explore.
Anyway, I have already
said too much and kept
you all too long, I'm afraid."

Sheila Declares Herself in Maternity!

The concluding segment provides a happy ending to the book and a new beginning for our protagonist-couple— Sheila finds herself pregnant with their first baby.

375
Sheila wanted to be sure
before sharing the news
with Vijay. She ran the
recommended tests,
in the privacy of her *boudoir,*
renewing her acquaintance
with light-blue litmus
paper she last touched
in college chemistry.
"Dip it in the solution, but
let it not sink. Wait for
a minute, and see if it turns pink!"
instructed Rajni, confidant
and conception consultant.
Sheila, her hand trembling,
followed the directions.
After waiting for what seemed
an eternity, she blushed and
declared herself in maternity!

376
"Mummy, I've some good
news for you!" confided Sheila,
into the cordless.
"Oh, really, *puttu*? My darling,

congratulations!" cooed Shobha
Murthy, into her handset
(courtesy: Bangalore Telephones).
"*Amma*, I didn't even tell you
what it is, and you're all excited.
You see, Vijay and I are going
to have a *baby*!" Sheila blurted out.
"I knew it, *puttu*. What else could it be
that you'll call me about,
at this ungodly hour! Speaking of
God, I've been praying *Nanjundappa*—
he has obviously answered!
Your father will be thrilled
to hear this," Shobha declared.
Sheila smiled, thinking of
her *Nanjundappa*, slaving away
in his American prison!

377
Sheila debated whether to call
Vijay at work, and distract
him from serious matters,
or wait till the evening.
She decided to wait.
She walked into the kitchen,
and surveyed the stores.
Good—she had everything,
for *Kesri Baath*. She fried
the *soji* in a pan, till
golden brown. Next, she
sauteed some cashews and red
raisins in butter; she then
mixed the nuts and
raisins into the *soji*,

and put in a cup of cane sugar;
on a whim, added some more;
last, but not the least,
a pinch of saffron.
She then stirred the admixture
in boiling water, after
throwing in a stick of butter.
It tasted *divine!*
Still, it's only 2 o'clock...
378
Vijay walked in, at last,
jingling car keys and carrying
the paper. "Anyone home?
I smell something good...
Is it sweet *Kesri*?" he queried.
"Yes, we're home, and yes,
it's sweet *Kesri*!"
Sheila replied sweetly.
"Oh, you have company?"
Vijay looked around,
looking for a Nalini
or Rajni.
"Yes, dear daddy,
you and I now have company!"
Sheila said coyly.
"You don't say! Really, Shiloo?
How do you know? Have you
been to the doctor? Tell me,
is it a boy or girl?
Wow, I'm thrilled!"

379
"Take it easy, silly!
You can't tell it's

a boy or girl, not yet.
All I know is another little
soul decided to join us—
you and I—in this
two-room townhouse!"
said Sheila, putting things
in perspective. Vijay was
hardly listening—he was ecstatic.
You can't go wrong with either.
If it's a girl, she'll be
pretty, with big wide eyes,
just like Sheila, and smart, to boot.
In case it's a boy,
why, it'll be down my alley!
We'll play and we'll fuss,
which will be lovely.

380
They talked late into the night,
making plans and modifying
them in midstream.
Vijay went online,
and checked out nifty names
for little Indian babes.
"You see, a child's name
is an important thing.
He'll carry it with him, all
his life. It's his handle—
you want to be sure
you aren't saddling him
with a teaser.
American schoolyards
are notoriously rowdy;
why, of all people,

you ought to know..."
Vijay lectured, protectively.
Sheila grew exasperated.
"Will you stop? Anyway,
why are you presuming
it'll be a boy? What's it called,
narcissism? I don't want
another male chauvinist
around!" Sheila put her
swollen foot down.

381
On and on, they go,
living their dreams,
actualizing their
aspirations—man, woman,
and child.
There'll be
more to come. Mostly mundane,
and predictable. Safe, sound,
and secure, for the most part.
They will have their trying
times, for sure, with means to
overcome, thanks to the
super-organized American society,
designed for order, within its borders.
Planned Obsolescence, perhaps,
but the alternative is alarming.
It's a grace
to grow old gracefully
and go away hand-in-hand...

Author's Afterword

America Attraction is a real thing. Many around the world experience the pull some time or the other, whether or not they actually make the move. This book tries to portray what awaits the visitor in the "destination nation", how he/she typically reacts and how, over time, one is invariably transformed by the place—"transmogrified into an all-business-American."

This book was conceived in my mind around the millennium, written and completed over the following decade. After a few half-hearted attempts at having it published, I shelved the manuscript. At long last, my writing is seeing the light of day now, in 2025, thanks mainly to the proactive and conducive publishing environment now prevalent.

A convergence of circumstances prompted me to write the book: America had met all the expectations I had brought with me from India, and more. Suffice to say, I happened to be well prepared when I arrived, able to 'join and merge into the American traffic' fairly easily. Quite early, I was struck by how big the country was and how varied the social conditions. The fact that I chose employment as a professional psychologist working in high security prisons, and thereby thrust myself right away into "the underbelly of America," to put it starkly, probably accounts for my impression. You can see how the character of Dr. Vijay Bhaskar might have been stirring inside me already. Believe it or not, at about the same time, Sheila Bhaskar, the other protagonist, was also making her presence felt inside my creative space! This is because, in addition to my prison job, I was also working as a part-time consultant in the local schools, interacting with the students and their teachers. While the fictional character Sheila in our fantasy was assigned to teach math, in my case, I was providing psychological services in the schools, "very much in the flesh."

How did I manage, walking straight into such forbidding and weighty assignments, soon after arriving? Speaking the language was key—fortunately, I was already oriented to Americanisms and colloquial expressions. All the American magazines, cartoons, and books I used to read as a youngster in India, and the Hollywood matinees I cut classes to watch, had turned me into an America aficionado, without me realizing it. Another significant factor at play was my military experience—I was a commissioned officer in the Indian Army and saw combat duty in India. I needed that and more to enter and work in the daunting, high-security American prisons! Working as a psychologist with children and young people in urban schools presented me with a different kind of challenge. Trying to accomplish all this as "a fresh-off-the-boat," to use a picturesque American expression, forced me to acculturate quickly. So there you have it—you can see how the material for the two main characters in *Vijay & Sheila,* was thrust in front of me, very early.

Do books go stale? Reading the book, written several years ago, readers might find some of the cultural and commercial references to be quaint, even nostalgic. By the same token, the keen reader would also realize that the book is actually about more enduring things— nothing less than the culture and character of America and Americans. Just as in the case of people, nations are also fallible, except, in the case of the United States, the country happens to be constantly self-correcting and seeking to improve itself.

It is important to add that the book celebrates not only American culture, but equally language, words, and sounds. Some things do have a long shelf life.

Glossary and Helpful Notes

ABCD: American-born Confused Deshi—a teasing reference to the youth of Indian origin, who were born and raised in the US.
Aloo Gobhi: a popular potato-cauliflower dish.
Ayyo: gesture of exclamation.
Ayyo, deva: Oh, Lord!
Ayyo, Paapu: Oh, poor thing!
Barfi: A North Indian sweet, made of sugar and dairy.
Bengali: person belonging to the Indian state of Bengal, criss-crossed with rivers and waterways.
Bhakti: An attitude and path of devotion to God
Bhogi: one who seeks luxury and comforts.
Bobbattu (same as Vobbattu): a flat, round, and stuffed dessert.
Bisi Bele Baath: a very spicy and hot preparation, made with rice.
Brindavan: The playground of Lord Krishna in Hindu Mythology.
Carnatic: Ancient, classical music system of South India.
Chappals: Sandals
Chennagide: Very nice (Kannada)
Chutney: A dip or relish
Chhat: A special snack, containing a heavy mixture of spices.
Dakshin Khand: Southern India
Deshi: a native or citizen of India

Dravidian: A native of Southern India, a descendent of the indigenous people.

Draupadi: Also, Draupathi, a female character from the epic, *Maha Bharatha,* who was spared from public disrobement and embarrassment, when her sari was magically rendered eternally long, thanks to Lord Krishna's magical intervention.

Drone: a steady, repetitive, background musical sound provided by a tambura or even an electrical device.

Filmi: relating to cinema or films

Gaathram: the gift of voice, having to do with vocalization.

Ganesh: a popular Indian deity: half-elephant, half-human.

Hangama: hullabaloo; hubbub

Halal: ritualized practice of Muslim butchers, similar to kosher.

Happla: circular, thin, crunchy snacks, which are spicy and deep-fried.

Hara: another name for the Hindu god, Shiva

Hari: Hindu god, Vishnu

Harijan: a child of God.

Hatha Yogi: a practitioner of Hatha Yoga, a rigorous form of physical yoga practice involving contortions and postures.

Hudigi: a girl (Kannada)

High Funda: able and bright—skilled in fundamentals (youthful slang)

Idli: steamed cakes, made from lentil/rice batter.

Jari: metallic adornment, on the borders of silk saris

Kaala Bhairav: another 'version' of the god, Shiva

Karma /Karmic: the Hindu philosophical term for fate or destiny.

Kelsa: relating to one's job or employment

Keshav: another name for Lord Vishnu

Kesri Baath: a preparation flavored by saffron.

Kurta-Pajama: typical casual garments worn by Indian males.

Lal Bagh: is a centrally located garden-park in the city of Bangalore.

Laksha Dweep: literally one hundred thousand tiny islands off the southern tip of India, in the Arabian Sea.

Mahatma: An evolved or great soul of a person

Madhav: Lord Krishna, who plays a central role in *The Maha Bharath.*

Masala: mixture of hot spices; a potpourri

Masuranna: a mixture of yogurt and rice—a common dish in South India

Mridangam: Indigenous drums from South India, a counterpart of the *Tabla.*

Mulligatawny: an anglicized reference to *Molaga Tanni (*Tamil), a thin soup made with peppers popular in the city of Madras, and the Tamilnadu state of India.

Muni: a sage, a hermit

Namaskar/Namasthe: a common Indian greeting

Praana/Prana: Life force of the individual

Prarabdha: Similar to the Hindu concept of Karma, having to do with reaping the fruits of one's actions from past lives.

Purandara: a well-known South Indian music composer from the past

Pushkar: a Hindu river-based festival, observed every 12 years.

Puttu: the little one, an endearment used towards children (Kannada)

Rama/Ram: the heroic god figure from the epic *Ramayana*—now a common Indian name.

Ram Navami: a nine-day festival in honor of Lord Rama.

Raag/Raagam: a musical scale, a main feature of classical Indian music.

Raagam, Taanam, Pallavi: three elements of the Carnatic music system.

Rosgolla: a spongy sweet made of dairy, popular in Calcutta, and the Indian state of Bengal.

Saambar: a thick spicy soup of vegetables from Southern India

Salwar: baggy female pajamas/trousers.

Samosa: a popular stuffed snack, goes well with hot tea

Samsara: The worldly journey; life of the householder.

Sari: the traditional dress for Indian women

Sa ri ga ma pa: Part of the basic musical Octave in Indian classical music.

Shambho: another name for Shiva

Shankara: another name for Shiva

Shiv Ling: The cylindrical symbol, representing Shiva's "sacred phallus."

Shiv Shakti: The Power of Shiva
Sholapuri: having to do with the Indian city Sholapur, famous for its leather sandals.
Shraddha: to be devoted to the task at hand, diligence
Sitar: a stringed instrument from North India.
Soji: cream of wheat
Stothram: chanting, in praise of God.
Surya Namaskar: "salutations to the Sun", yoga postures, at dawn.
Swaram: tone; musical sound
Tabla/Tablaist: Percussion or percussionist in Indian music
Tahini: a middle-eastern, ground-sesame item
Thayi: mother (kannada)
Thayappa: a common name
Thyagaraja/Thyagayya: a famous and prolific composer of Carnatic music.
TLC: American abbreviation for tender loving care.
Upma/Uppittu: a South Indian dish, made of cream of wheat/rice.
Vadai: a popular South Indian savory donut
Vedic: pertaining to the Vedas—ancient scriptures of India.
Veena: a stringed instrument from South India, counterpart of the North Indian Sitar.
Varnam: a musical term, related to the raagam
Vishnu: One of the Hindu Divine Trinity—Brahma, Vishnu, and Shiva.

Vaishnavite: any one, belonging to the Vishnu sect of Brahmins.

Vobbattu: same as Bobbattu, described above.

Yaga/Yagna: an involved, religious ritual from ancient times.

Yaar: a term of endearment (Hindi)

www.ingramcontent.com/pod-product-compliance
Lightning Source LLC
Chambersburg PA
CBHW070908120626
46546CB00001B/177